THE IMMINENT SECOND COMING

LEWIS S. BROWNLOW

ISBN: 978-1-4669-5353-6 (sc)
ISBN: 978-1-4669-5352-9 (e)

Trafford rev. 09/12/2012

 www.trafford.com

North America & international
toll-free: 1 888 232 4444 (USA & Canada)
phone: 250 383 6864 ♦ fax: 812 355 4082

CONTENTS

LIST OF FIGURES

INTRODUCTION

This book approaches the subject of the second coming from some unusual angles. Pyramids, star alignments, the constellation of Orion, the Shepherd Stone of Israel, the Temple at Jerusalem and Adam-Ondi-Ahman all feature in this book along with other fascinating and unusual indicators.

One good reason to study the signs of the times is so that we can be adequately prepared for the troubled times that will precede the Second Coming of The Saviour. In the Pearl of Great Price (Smith, The Pearl of Great Price, 1851), the Saviour tells us that the faithful will be alerted to the nearness of His coming by the signs of the times. Joseph Smith Matthew 1:37-39:

> 37 And whoso treasureth up my word, shall not be deceived, for the Son of Man shall come, and he shall send his angels before him with the great sound of a trumpet, and they shall gather together the remainder of his elect from the four winds, from one end of heaven to the other.
>
> 38 Now learn a parable of the fig tree—When its branches are yet tender, and it begins to put forth leaves, you know that summer is nigh at hand;
>
> 39 So likewise, mine elect, when they shall see all these things, they shall know that he is near, even at the doors;

So the faithful Saints will be warned of the Saviour's impending second coming. But will they be warned of the start of the upheavals of nature which will precede the second coming? I believe the answer is yes, but only if they watch the signs of the times carefully.

Some of the signs of the second coming that are indicated in this book are different to the more commonly referenced signs. That they involve symbolism should not be a surprise to the reader since the Lord has clearly used symbolism throughout the scriptures and in the decoration on his Temples. Although some of the signs are out of the ordinary, they nevertheless point to the same conclusion as do the more usual signs and they do so, arguably, with more immediacy. There will, no doubt, be people who consider that some of the signs in this book are somewhat speculative. I do not deny this. I am not a professional academic bound by the chains of a reputation dependent upon not publishing anything that cannot be verified and backed up by numerous references. However, I have provided a reasonable number of references and I believe the breadth of the topics and the cumulative weight of the evidences given, even if one or two are dismissed as too speculative, is convincing. Some constructive speculation is sometimes necessary in order to advance the boundaries of knowledge.

To be able to appreciate the signs in the first part of this book requires some small explanation of Egyptian pyramids and star alignments, but if the reader will patiently grasp the explanations given, the reward is great indeed! Later chapters look at some signs from a Jewish perspective, from political and economic perspectives and from an historical perspective. The signs may come from radically different backgrounds but they all unify in one shout—the tribulations which will come upon the world preceding the second coming of Christ are imminent! This book is a salutary warning to be prepared!

CH 1

Pyramids and the Puzzle of the Empty Sarcophagi

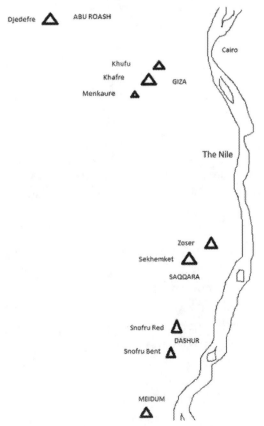

Figure 1—The Main Pyramids of Egypt

The first pyramid of any note was built at Saqqara during the reign of Zoser in the third dynasty of Egyptian pharaohs. Previous to that, pharaohs had built mastabas or burial mounds/tombs on a smaller scale.

Dynasty	Pharaoh	Pyramid
	Zanakht	
	Zoser	Yes
	Sekhemket	Yes
	Khaba	
	Nebka	
Third (Around 2700 BC)	Huni	
	Snofru	Two
	Khufu	Yes
	Djedefre	Yes
	Khafre	Yes
	MenKaure	Yes
Fourth (Around 2600 BC)	Shepseskaf	

Figure 2—The Third and Fourth Dynasties of Egypt

Zoser's pyramid was a step pyramid with six giant steps including a flat top. Its building was probably supervised by the great vizier Imhotep. The Egyptians had built in stone before—indeed some stone mastabas were built. However, the building of the step pyramid of Zoser represented an order of magnitude advance in both organisational skills and in building techniques. Zoser's pyramid was first built with four steps before being enlarged to its final six steps. It has been calculated that the final six step pyramid contains over 800,000 tons of quarried and dressed limestone. Hence the organisational skills needed to manage a sufficient labour force to accomplish the quarrying, dressing, transporting and building must have been substantial. It was project management on a large scale even by today's standards. In addition, the building skills required were considerable since the weight of the stone in a large pyramid is enormous and trouble has to be taken to avoid the build up of lateral forces which would destroy the pyramid catastrophically. The stone has to be accurately dressed, particularly in the horizontal plane, in order to keep the forces vertical. Also, the step pyramid was not built as an amorphous mass inside the stepped shell. There are a series of inward leaning buttress walls around a central core (see Figure 3) and this ingenious technique employed by Imhotep renders the tall pyramid shape safe from collapse under its own weight. The buttress walls get shorter as they progress from the centre to the outside of the pyramid to fit the stepped shape.

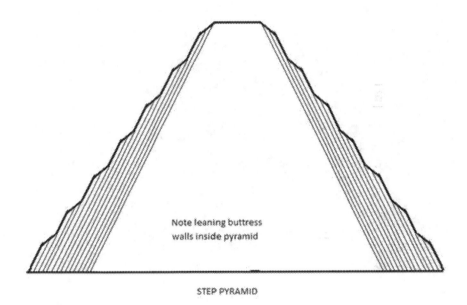

Note leaning buttress walls inside pyramid

STEP PYRAMID

Figure 3—The Step Pyramid with its Buttress Walls

An unfinished pyramid nearby Zoser's appears to be of similar construction and to relate to his successor Sekhemket. It only reached around seven metres high but the buttress walls were present showing that pyramids were built from the ground up rather than from the centre outwards. Pyramids always have a passage (or passages) leading under or into the structure, usually with a chamber at the end. An unopened sarcophagus was found in that of Sekhemket provoking much excitement. However, when it was opened it proved to be completely empty.

Subsequent to the step pyramids at Saqqara, attempts were made to further refine the step shape by clothing it in a shell of dressed stone which would give a true pyramidal shape. The pyramid at Meidum was the first attempt. Unfortunately, the shell of dressed stone was not fixed securely enough and a catastrophic collapse occurred during building. The results can be seen in figure 4 with the step pyramid shape remaining but with the debris from the collapse of the smooth shell surrounding it. Excavations have revealed the bottom few layers of the dressed stone shell remaining attached to the step pyramid under the debris. Kurt Mendelssohn explains the details of this collapse in his book 'The Riddle of the Pyramids'. (Mendelssohn, 1974)

Figure 4—The Collapsed Meidum Pyramid

Mendelssohn suggests that at the time of the collapse of the Meidum pyramid, which was being built at an approximate angle of 52 degrees to the vertical, the so called 'Bent' pyramid was also under construction at the same angle. In order to avoid another potential collapse, the builders lowered the angle on the upper section to around 43½ degrees thus giving the 'bent' profile.

The next pyramid to be built was the 'Red' pyramid (so called because of the reddish hue of its stone). It was built entirely at the lower angle 43½ degrees—the same as the upper portion of the bent pyramid—presumably for the same reason.

A pyramid with an angle of elevation of 52 degrees (51 degrees 52 minutes to be more exact) has a remarkable geometrical property. The ratio of the height of the pyramid to the circumference of its base is the same as the ratio of the radius to the circumference of a circle—i.e. ½π.

The next large pyramid to be built—the 'Great Pyramid' of Khufu at Giza near Cairo was the zenith of pyramid building. It is the largest pyramid in Egypt and was built with a smooth dressed limestone shell at an angle which fitted the ratio mentioned above to one part in a thousand. This is too accurate to be a coincidence and shows purpose in the building. The pyramid has many passages and chambers including a passage which points at the pole star (most pyramids have this feature). When it was first completed, it must have been a spectacular sight shimmering white in the bright Egyptian sunlight and with its capstone painted gold. The pyramid has several passages and chambers and the large chamber called the King's chamber contains an empty sarcophagus. The sarcophagus must have been placed there during the building of the pyramid since it is too large to fit down the connecting passages. Most of the dressed limestone shell of the pyramid has been stolen by later builders for other buildings around Cairo. The large granite blocks that form the true pyramidal shape (presumably on top of the buttressed step pyramid underneath) remain. All pyramids were built as step pyramids first before having a smooth shell fitted over since it would be impossible to keep all four corners of the shell straight and meeting at a point without this intermediate form. When the stepped pyramid was complete, a sighting rod was erected in the centre of the top step reaching up to where the point of the pyramid would be. The corners of the shell were then sighted onto the top of the rod as they were built.

Khufu's pyramid at Giza was followed by a small pyramid built further North at Abu Roash by Djedefre.

The next pyramid at Giza was Khafre's, which actually looks higher than Khufu's since it was built on elevated ground, but which is actually slightly smaller than Khufu's. It is not as carefully built as Khufu's pyramid though it retains some of its limestone shell towards the top. Khafre's pyramid has only one small chamber underneath it with two entrance passages.

The small pyramid at Giza is that of Menkaure and it has three chambers underneath with an entrance passage. A sarcophagus and mummy were found in one of the chambers but although the coffin lid had Menkaure's name on it, it dated to a late dynastic age. The mummy dated even later—to the early Christian era AD. Pyramid building then went into decline. Some pyramids were built by later dynasties but they were generally small or of mud brick and not lasting.

"To suppose that the pyramid's only function in ancient Egypt was as a royal tomb, would be an oversimplification" wrote Miroslav Verner in '*The Pyramids*', p. 45 (Verner, 2001)

Pyramids are assumed by most people to have been intended as the tombs of the Kings/Pharaohs that had them built. However, there is no reliable evidence that any Pharaoh was ever buried in a pyramid! Many contain empty coffins/sarcophagi but there is no indication that the sarcophagi ever contained the mummies of the Pharaohs.

Vidler wrote (Vidler, 1998), "There is no decent physical evidence to demonstrate that any of them were ever buried in any pyramid—in fact not a single fingernail from a single Pharaoh has ever been recovered from any ancient pyramid!"

The robbers who broke into the Great Pyramid c 820 AD under Caliph Al Mamoun found to their great surprise that there was nothing whatever there, in the whole extent of the burial chamber, except an empty stone chest without a lid.

Dr Kurt Mendelsohn said, "While the funerary function of the pyramids cannot be doubted, it is rather more difficult to prove that the pharaohs were ever buried inside them." He also pointed out that, 'Whichever way we look at the problem, we cannot get away from the fact that for this period there exist more large pyramids than Pharaohs who could have been buried in them.' (Mendelssohn, 1974)

In short, the pyramids were not so much tombs with bodies as cenotaphs or centres for the funeral worship of the deceased Pharaohs. But did they also serve some other purpose?

Pyramid	Sarcophagi	Empty?
Zoser		Empty except for one foot
Sekhemket	1	Sealed and empty
Meidum		
Bent		
Red		
Khufu	1	No lid and empty
Djedefre		
Khafre	1	Empty
Menkaure	1	Sarcophagus sank at sea

Figure 5—Pyramids and their Contents

The list above shows that the pyramids and sarcophagi were almost all empty with the exception of that of Zoser which contained one mummified foot. We would like to say that Zoser had 'one foot in the grave', but it is not certain whose foot it was nor is it certain that the tomb was intended as his grave! The empty burial chambers and sarcophagi in the pyramids could be explained as being the result of tomb robbing. However, some of the chambers (e.g., that of Sekhemket and one under the step pyramid) were undisturbed since antiquity when discovered, so this suggests that these tombs never contained a body or mummy. When we add to this the fact that some pharaohs had more than one pyramid or tomb,—e.g. Snofru, and could not therefore have been buried in more than one of them, we begin to realise that the pyramids may have been more funerary monuments than tombs.

On a stone stela at Abydos, pharaoh Ahmose states that he wishes to make a pyramid for his mother queen Tetisheri, who was already deceased, despite the fact that she already had tombs in Thebes and Abydos. Clearly the queen could not be buried in all three tombs and therefore we are forced to the conclusion that these pyramids and tombs were more memorials or cenotaphs than burial places.

But were the empty sarcophagi symbolic in any way? Were they intended to convey any ideas to visitors? Were they supposed to indicate or be evidence that the Pharaoh concerned had risen from the tomb and had been resurrected as had their God Osiris? The Egyptians believed their Pharaohs were divine and had godlike qualities and the Pharaohs wanted to perpetuate this belief. It is therefore very possible that the empty sarcophagi were supposed to indicate that the deceased pharaoh had been resurrected as Osiris had been according to Egyptian religious beliefs. This connection with Osiris will become more relevant when we see the Christian connection with Osiris in Chapter 3.

In the next chapter, we will look at the alignments of the main shafts of the Great Pyramid (Khufu's) with stars in the ancient sky and consider whether the alignment was by design.

CH 2

THE CONNECTIONS IN THE SKY

Some Egyptologists have suggested that the pyramid shafts were passages by which the king's soul could leave the pyramid to begin its journey to the sky. Later Egyptians represented the soul or ba of a person as a human-headed bird which could explain the size of the shafts. The fact that at least some of the shafts were blocked is not a problem for this interpretation as the Egyptians often carved a stone false door in tombs to represent a point of communication between the world of the living and the realms of the dead. A transfigured spirit could pass through such obstacles. This theory was widely accepted among Egyptologists at one time, although it does not explain why more than one shaft was necessary.

In 1964, Egyptologist Alexander Badawy and astronomer Virginia Trimble suggested that the shafts were oriented toward stars such as those of Orion's Belt and alpha-Draconis which was the closest star to the celestial pole at the time the pyramids were built. Computers allow us to calculate the position of the stars in antiquity and see which stars the shafts would have pointed at. The shafts are not straight and the stars would therefore not have been visible through them, but this does not preclude the idea that they were intended to direct the soul toward specific destinations. Indeed, about 110 years ago in his book 'The Dawn of Astronomy', Sir Norman Lockyer suggested, 'It is not impossible that some of the mysterious passages to be found in the pyramid of Khufu may have some astronomical use'. (Lockyer, 1894)

Nowadays, most experts accept that at least some of the shafts in the great pyramid were designed to point to the stars in some way. But in what way did they point?

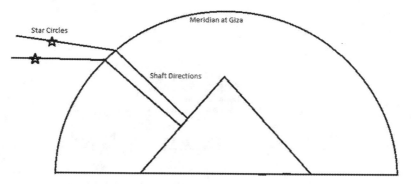

Figure 6—The Alignment of a Shaft and a Star

All the angled shafts in the Great Pyramid pointed at different positions in the sky (or on the celestial sphere that can be imagined to surround the Earth and on which all stars can be mapped). However, all the shafts pointed at one line of longitude on the celestial sphere. It was the meridian which passed through Giza.

As the Earth rotates, the stars describe circles in the sky at the particular latitude of their position on the celestial sphere. A star is considered to be aligned with a shaft or other angle when its circle crosses the meridian of the Great Pyramid at the same point as the extended shaft direction intersects it. What is more, if more than one star crosses the meridian at that point, the brightest star crossing at that point is considered to be the 'aligned star'. This is the convention followed by Badawy and Trimble.

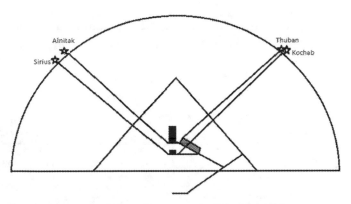

**Figure 7—The Alignments of the Four Main
Shafts of the Great Pyramid of Khufu**

In 'The Orion Mystery' (Bauval, 1994), Bauval and Gilbert showed how the main shafts of the Great Pyramid were aligned on the meridian with the first four bright stars shown in Figure 7 around the time 2450 BC. All four stars pointed at by the shafts were significant to the ancient Egyptians. Thuban was the pole star. Kochab was in the Little Bear constellation and appeared in Egyptian drawings. Alnitak was the brightest star in Orion's belt. Sirius symbolised Isis the sister and wife of Osiris the Egyptian god. For all four shafts to align with significant stars is unlikely to have happened by chance. Further, Vidler in 'The Star Mirror (Vidler, 1998)' has shown that seven other significant directions in the pyramid such as the North and South faces also aligned with bright stars around 2450 BC. For all these directions to align is most unlikely to have happened by chance. It indicates that the great pyramid was probably designed to synchronise with those star alignments at that date.

2450BC

Shaft etc	Pyramid Elevation Angle	Declination on Celestial Sphere	Star Alignment
Queen's Chamber Southern	39° 30'	-20° 31'	Sirius
King's Chamber Southern	45°	-15° 01'	Alnitak
Queen's Chamber Northern	39°	80° 59'	Kochab
King's Chamber Northern	32° 29'	87° 31'	Thuban
The North Face Angle	51° 51'	-08° 10'	Bellatrix
The South Face Angle	51° 51'	68° 08'	Yildun

Figure 8—The Main Alignments of Stars in 2450BC

It has also been suggested that the three pyramids at Giza represent the three stars in Orion's belt in relative position and magnitude, albeit in mirror image.

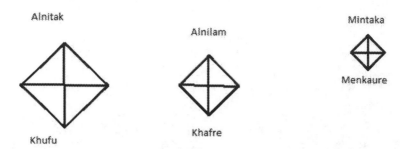

Figure 9—The Pyramids at Giza as Symbolic of the Stars of Orion's Belt

The alignments in figure 8 are given as at 2450 BC. The reason that a date is given for the alignments of the stars is because the alignments of stars change slowly over time due to the phenomenon of precession. Precession causes the constellations in the sky to rise and fall as if they were on heavenly waves which ebb and flow over thousands of years. Precession is a gravity induced, slow and continuous change in the orientation of the rotational axis of an astronomical body (in this case the Earth) with respect to the stars. This is sometimes called the 'Precession of the Equinoxes' since the equinoxes move westward along the ecliptic relative to the fixed stars whereas the Sun moves eastward. The ecliptic is the plane in which the Earth orbits the Sun (as seen below in Figure 10)

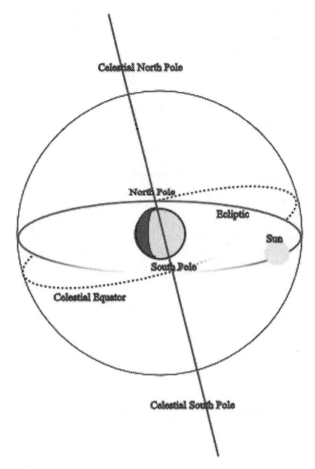

Figure 10—The Ecliptic and the Celestial Sphere

Precession can be thought of being like the wobbling of a spinning top when it is disturbed in its motion. The Earth spins on its axis of rotation, which passes through the poles, such that it completes one rotation in one day of approximately twenty four hours. However, its axis of rotation 'wobbles' or moves such that the poles describe two circles and the axis of rotation maps out a double cone shape. The upper cone is indicated in the figure below.

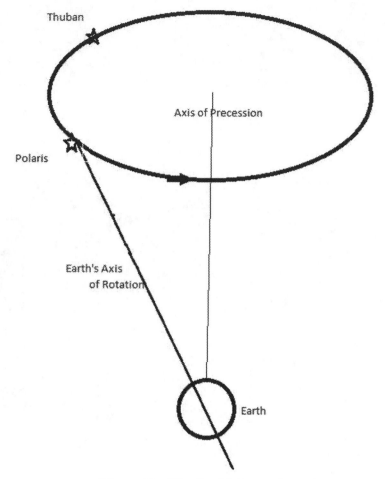

Figure 11—The Earth's Precession

This precessional rotation takes approx 26,000 years to complete one whole cycle or rotation. Thus its effects are not very noticeable in one lifetime but, over many generations, its effects are very obvious.

So, if the shafts of the great pyramid were designed to point to certain stars at the time of building of the great pyramid, they will not point to those stars now. We have to imagine the stars moved back through time to the time of building of the great pyramid (around 2450BC) to see where they pointed. Fortunately, some astronomical software programs allow us to visualise the night sky under this reversal of time.

The effects of precession are that the poles of the Earth appear to move in circles against the fixed background of the stars. So whereas the

North Pole pointed to Thuban in 2450BC, it now points to Polaris in the current era. In between these two times, it did not point to any major star. Another effect of precession is that the position of the Sun, relative to the stars, at the vernal equinox slowly regresses through the full 360 degrees crossing all the constellations of the zodiac. Hence we speak of different 'ages' such as the 'age of Aquarius' meaning the age when the sun at the vernal equinox is in Aquarius. This constant slow movement of the Earth with respect to the stars underlines just how unlikely it is that all the shafts and angles of the Great Pyramid should align by accident with major stars at any one time.

To sum up this chapter so far, we have outlined how stars can be 'pointed to' or 'aligned with' the direction of the shafts of the great pyramid. We have also described the phenomenon of precession and how it changes the relative position of stars with respect to the Earth over time. Given this changing relative position of the stars, it is clearly extremely unlikely that all the shafts and angles of the great pyramid would align with major stars at any one time. However, in 2450 BC that is exactly what they did. The question that can now be asked is, 'Have the shafts and angles of the great pyramid lined up synchronously with major stars at any other time since 2450 BC and will they do so in the future?'

We have explained that, as a result of the phenomenon of 'precession', all stars move uniformly with respect to the Earth over a long period of time. The pole star now is Polaris, the brightest star that ever hovers above the North Pole. Clearly the shaft of the great pyramid that pointed to Thuban in 2450BC now points to Polaris, 4460 years later. In between those two dates, there was no major star at the pole and therefore the shaft concerned did not point to any major star in between those two dates. So we can confidently state that there has not been an asynchronous alignment of the major shafts of the great pyramid with major stars between 2450 BC and the present date (2012).

However, as mentioned above, the King's Chamber Northern shaft which pointed to Thuban in 2450 BC now points to Polaris the pole star. But do the other shaft alignments point to anything now? Yes! They point to other major stars in the sky. In fact the major directions of the Great Pyramid synchronously align with the directions of major stars best at around 2040 AD. This is far too much of an unlikely coincidence to be pure chance. In between these two dates (2450 BC and 2040 AD) there was no date at which the major directions of the Great Pyramid synchronously aligned with major stars. The table below gives details of which stars will align in 2040 AD:

Shaft etc	Pyramid Elevation Angle	Declination on Celestial Sphere	Star Alignment
Queen's Chamber Southern Shaft	39° 30'	-20° 31'	Beta Lupus (Nihal)
King's Chamber Southern	45°	-15° 01'	Gamma Librae
Queen's Chamber Northern	39°	80° 59'	HD8181 Draconis
King's Chamber Northern	32° 29'	87° 31'	Polaris
The North Face Angle	51° 51'	-08° 10'	Rigel
The South Face Angle	51° 51'	68° 08'	Rho Draconis

Figure 12—The Main Star Alignments in 2040 AD

Bearing in mind the extremely unlikely nature of such a second synchronism, we must ask ourselves whether the ancient builders of the great pyramid were trying to tell us something. Perhaps that the age in which we live is a special one in some way? If the shaft alignments with major stars are not a coincidence, and it is most unlikely that they are, then they must have been intentional and they must have been based on a knowledge of astronomy and perhaps of future events. But to what fairly imminent but still future event were the ancient Egyptians trying to draw our attention?

Before considering the answer to this question any further, we need to look at any connections or equivalencies between ancient Egyptian religion and Christianity.

CH 3

THE CHRISTIAN IDENTITY OF OSIRIS

Before investigating more closely what imminent but future event the ancient Egyptians were pointing at in the design of the Great Pyramid, we need to look at whether there is a connection between Egyptian religious beliefs and those of Christianity.

The central theme of Christianity is the atoning sacrifice of Jesus Christ in Gethsemane and on the cross at Calvary followed by His subsequent resurrection. Christ thereby conquered death and offered both resurrection and repentance to all.

A search of Egyptian religious beliefs on the internet reveals that:

'Osiris is the ancient Egyptian God who, like Christ, is the King in Heaven where souls go after death. Osiris, like Christ, is a God who goes before us to taste death but who returns to assure us of our resurrection'. Also, Osiris is the judge of the dead.

In the ancient Egyptian religion, the god Horus is sometimes referred to as the 'Sun of God'. However, there is often confusion between Horus and Osiris, who is sometimes implied to be Horus from a different perspective. Osiris is the god Horus after he died and was resurrected. Osiris is the King of Egypt, just as Christ is the King of the Jews. Osiris is murdered by his wicked brother Set (or Seth), who is the equivalent of Satan. The historian Dr Philip Myers compared Seth to Satan as the personification of evil whilst Osiris was the personification of good.

The famous Egyptologist Budge said that the Egyptians were well prepared to become Christians in that they saw Osiris as a prototype of Christ and Isis and her suckling child Horus as a prototype of the Virgin Mary with her infant child. Many people who have studied the Egyptian religion have commented on its similarities to Christianity e.g. Massey (Massey, 1907) and Witt (Witt, 1997).

An internet search of material on Egyptian religion reveals that Horus/Osiris:

1. Had a birth celebrated at the winter solstice.
2. Was killed through treachery.
3. Was of royal lineage with a mother Isis-Mery.
4. Was baptised at 30 years of age.
5. Was baptised by Anup the baptizer who was beheaded.
6. Had cruciform symbols (the Djed column and the Ankh).
7. Had twelve helpers or disciples.
8. Performed miracles.
9. Was crucified.
10. Was buried for three days and was resurrected as Osiris.
11. Was referred to as 'The Good Shepherd', 'The Lamb of God', 'The Messiah' and 'The Son of Man'.
12. Was the 'anointed one' and as Osiris was the 'KRST'.
13. Was to reign for one thousand years.

Thus, in many ways, Horus/Osiris of the Egyptians parallels Christ of the Christians.

Isis-Mery was referred to by Egyptians as 'neter mut' or 'Mother of God'. She was often said to be a virgin. These are clearly parallels with Mary the mother of Jesus Christ. The epithet 'Mery' often ascribed to Isis meant 'beloved'. This title has also been applied to Mary the mother of Jesus and indeed the name Mary is said by some to derive from the Egyptian root Mry meaning 'beloved'.

At this point, we must pause in case any of our readers are beginning to think that Christianity is in some way derived from Egyptian religion as suggested by some. They reach this conclusion as they believe Egyptian religion and beliefs predated Christianity. However, we must point out that the Gospel plan was known from before the beginning of man's time on the Earth. Adam knew about and understood the Gospel plan before he came to Earth and so did subsequent patriarchs. Christ and his mission were preached by prophets long before He came to Earth e.g.

In the Bible:
    Isaiah 53, Psalm 22, Isaiah 7:14, Isaiah 9:6,
    In the Book of Mormon (Smith, The Book of Mormon, 1830)
    2 Nephi 19:6, 2 Nephi 21:1, Jacob 4: 4-5, Mosiah 3, etc

It should be no surprise to us that the ancient Egyptians had a corrupt form of this Gospel. Indeed, as Nibley points out in his book 'The Message of the Joseph Smith Papyri' (Nibley, 1975) they even had a corrupt form of the Temple endowment ceremony. What might surprise some is the amount of detail that they knew about Christ's life but, as Isaiah reveals, the events of Christ's life were known in advance in great detail. The nature of His mission and the necessity of His fulfilling prophecy made this inevitable.

Some say that Osiris's birth was announced by three stars, Mintaka, Anilam and Alnitak which form Orion's belt. These three stars point in a line to Sirius (Sothis to Egyptians) the indicator of his birth. This is compared to the three wise men (magi) who came to see Jesus after His birth. The soul or Sahu of Osiris was said to dwell in the constellation Orion. The three stars in Orion's belt have been called the three kings.

Like many ancient religions, Egyptian religious rites commenced with ritual washings for purification purposes. These were akin to the baptism ordinance of Christian beliefs. According to the Egyptologist Gardiner, the ritual washing was the means of initiation into a properly legitimated religious life just as baptism serves a similar purpose for Christians. Anubis or Anup the baptizer was the Egyptian equivalent of John the Baptist in Christian beliefs. In 'The Book of the Dead' BD97, Horus approaches Anubis and says, "Lo I come, that I may purify this soul of mine in the most high degree'. This is suggestive of baptism for the remission of sins as practised by Christians. In Egyptian religion, the double faced god Janus was sometimes identified with the god Anubis (Anup). Hence there could be a link between the name John (Janus) and Anup.

Figure 13—Priests Anointing and Purifying The Osiris

Osiris had as his twelve helpers the hours of the night or the twelve zodiacal signs. The venerable Bede represented the twelve apostles of Christianity as the zodiacal signs giving yet another similarity with ancient Egyptian religion.

Lundy in his book 'Monumental Christianity' (Lundy, 1876) states 'Horus is thus represented as a cross-like, young mummy figure, because he is the life-giving power of the sun, using his cross to produce life and joy; and he is thus a type of Christ, in His greater conflict with sin, Satan, and death, and his triumph through the Cross'. Here Horus/Osiris is described as cross-like or cruciform. The Ankh is the Egyptian sign of the cross symbolic of life as Christ gave us all resurrection and life through his sacrifice on the cross.

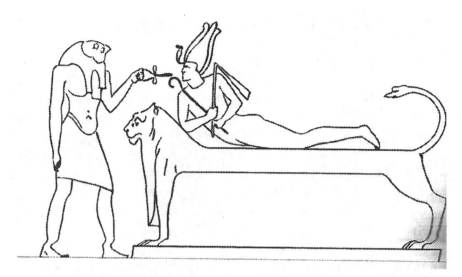

Figure 14—Horus Resurrecting the Deceased/Osiris Using the Ankh Cross

Lazarus, whom Jesus raised from the dead, has name similarities with the title often given to the deceased in Egypt viz. 'The Osiris'. In Arabic this would be rendered 'Al or El Osiris'. Lazarus is a Greek form equivalent to Eleazar in Hebrew which means 'whom God helps'. Another form of this is El Azar and indeed Bethany where the miracle of the raising of Lazarus took place is today called El Azarieh by the Arabs.

There is also a parallel between the story in Luke 16:20-25 and an Egyptian legend about Osiris and his son.

Murdock (Murdock, 2009) has pointed out that Osiris mummified is referred to as 'Osiris-Karast' and the mummy risen to its feet was Osiris 'krst', the anointed, embalmed one which is also transliterated sometimes as 'queres-t' or 'qrs.t'. As such he is a type of Christ whose name means 'the anointed one'. The Greek is Christos, the Latin Christus but both mean the anointed one. Krst in Egyptian can mean anointed or buried depending on the determinative used with it. Old Testament kings such as David and Solomon were often referred to in Greek as 'Christos' meaning that they were anointed (to be king).

In the Year (Sed) festival of the Egyptians, the ritual killing of the Pharaoh was acted out. (Sometimes some poor unfortunate was surreptitiously substituted for the Pharaoh at the last minute so that the death was real). The Pharaoh then miraculously came back to life and showed himself to the people, thus proving his godlike powers over death and becoming an 'Osiris'.

In summary, Christianity was neither new at the time of Christ's mission on Earth nor was it strange but it had existed from before the time of Adam. Indeed, Eusebius and Augustine had both admitted such in their writings. The plan of salvation had been revealed to man from the beginning including the need of a Redeemer and who it would be.

So, to re-iterate the main idea of this chapter, Osiris is the Egyptian equivalent of the Christian central figure Jesus Christ, i.e. CHRIST = OSIRIS. Osiris was a mythical figure who was symbolic of Christ or who was a 'type' of Christ. In writing or talking about Osiris, the Egyptians were effectively expressing their knowledge of what would happen to Christ but without realising it and without realising the full meaning of the knowledge which they had. As Nibley (Nibley, 1975) indicated, their religion was a corruption of the true Gospel.

Let us now see how this equivalency has implications when looking at the constellations and their symbolism.

CH 4

THE SIGN OF THE SON OF MAN

The constellation of Orion was symbolic of the God Osiris to the ancient Egyptians and, when called Sahu, represented the soul of Osiris. As Osiris of the Egyptians is equated with Christ of Christians, by extension or association then, Orion is one of the signs of Christ who is sometimes referred to as 'The Son of Man' by Christians. Hence the constellation of Orion could be considered to be one of the signs of the Son of Man. It is probably not the one grand sign of the second coming of the 'Son of Man' since Joseph Smith translated:

"Judah must return, Jerusalem must be rebuilt, and the temple, and water come out from under the temple, and the waters of the Dead Sea be healed [see Ezekiel]. It will take some time to rebuild the walls of the city and the temple, etc.; and all this must be done before the Son of Man will make His appearance. There will be wars and rumours of wars, signs in the heavens above and on the earth beneath, the sun turned into darkness and the moon to blood, earthquakes in divers places, the seas heaving beyond their bounds; then will appear one grand sign of the Son of Man in heaven. But what will the world do? They will say it is a planet, a comet, etc. But the Son of Man will come as the sign of the coming of the Son of Man, which will be as the light of the morning cometh out of the east." (Smith, Teachings of the Prophet Joseph Smith, 1976)

So one grand sign of the second coming of the Son of Man will be considered to be a planet or a comet by observers and the constellation of Orion does not fall into that category of occurrences. However, there is something interesting about the constellation of Orion that makes it a potential sign of the special nature of the current era in time and of the troubles which will affect the Earth prior to the second coming of Christ.

Like all other stars, the stars which constitute the Orion constellation are subject to precession and over time change their position in the sky. The effect is that Orion has been gradually rising in the sky since the pyramids were built and has now reached its zenith or highest position in the night sky. The raised limb of Orion (often considered to be a pointing finger) now points at a very special position in the sky. It is the place where the rising of the solstice sun on the ecliptic crosses the galactic (Milky Way) equator. (See Fig 15). This coincidence has not happened for 25,830 years (if indeed it has ever happened before!). In addition, the stars of Orion's belt just reach 0 degrees on the celestial equator and the stars of Orion's dagger (or phallus to some cultures) assume a straight line. This is a unique set of coincidences—so much so that one wonders whether it is indeed a coincidence or whether it was planned. Does it also indicate something very special about this era of time? The Great Pyramid clearly links to the constellation of Orion both in the fact that its shafts point to some of the stars of Orion and in that it forms, along with the other two Giza pyramids, a plan of the stars in the belt of Orion. Are both the constellation of Orion and the design of the Great Pyramid pointing at some anciently known truth about our special era of time?

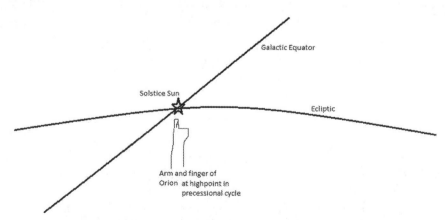

Figure 15—The Finger of Orion Pointing at the Solstice Sun

Also the constellation of Orion now rises over the Mount of Olives due East of the Jerusalem Temple mount at the summer solstice. This, of course, is where revelation has indicated that the Saviour Jesus Christ will return to Earth in glory at the second coming. Acts 1:9-12.

> 9 And when he had spoken these things, while they beheld, he was taken up; and a cloud received him out of their sight.
>
> 10 And while they looked stedfastly toward heaven as he went up, behold, two men stood by them in white apparel;
>
> 11 Which also said, Ye men of Galilee, why stand ye gazing up into heaven? this same Jesus, which is taken up from you into heaven, shall so come in like manner as ye have seen him go into heaven.
>
> 12 Then returned they unto Jerusalem from the mount called Olivet, which is from Jerusalem a Sabbath day's journey.

Also Zechariah 14:4 refers.

> 4 ¶And his feet shall stand in that day upon the mount of Olives, which *is* before Jerusalem on the east, and the mount of Olives shall cleave in the midst thereof toward the east and toward the west, *and there shall be* a very great valley; and half of the mountain shall remove toward the north, and half of it toward the south

So this sign could be another indicator of the special nature of this time in the age of man.

The main sign of the Son of Man spoken of by Joseph Smith as appearing as a comet or a planet will not occur until after the tribulations and upheavals of the Earth have subsided. It will probably appear after the silence in heaven which lasts for half an hour (see Ch 17). Joseph Smith Matthew 1:36 refers.

> 36 And, as I said before, after the tribulation of those days, and the powers of the heavens shall be shaken, **then** shall appear the sign of the Son of Man in heaven, and then shall

all the tribes of the earth mourn; and they shall see the Son of
Man coming in the clouds of heaven, with power and great
glory;

The Second Coming of the Lord will follow on from this sign,
probably fairly quickly.

CH 5

The Tomb of Seti I

Before leaving the world of the pyramids and constellations, there is one other clue in ancient Egypt of what might be special about the current era of time. In the tomb of Pharaoh Seti I in the Valley of the Kings, there is a mural on the ceiling of the tomb that has puzzled historians for centuries.

Figure 16—Sketch of Part of the Ceiling in the Tomb of Seti I

Fig 16 above represents a portion of this mural. The mural contains some of the constellations as known to the ancient Egyptians at the time it was drawn. In the picture we see Ra Herakty (the sun God) who appears to be holding the ecliptic or apparent path of the Sun as viewed from the Earth. A figure which represents Orion/Osiris (or Sahu their starry equivalent) stands under the ecliptic with its raised hand and finger pointing to the ecliptic. Remember we have already shown that Orion can be taken as a sign of Christ. At the precise point where the outstretched finger would touch the ecliptic, the ecliptic takes a sharp deviation from its normal path in the form of a loop. As explained in Ch 4, this is the current position of the sun at its summer solstice. The picture represents the sky at the present time! Orion, the sign of the Son of Man (Christ) is pointing at a change in the ecliptic or maybe a deviation in the Earth's orbital path!

Is it a coincidence that this configuration of the objects in the sky occurs just as the shafts of the Great Pyramid synchronize their directions on important stars? Were the ancient Egyptians trying to communicate an idea to us or pass on some of their sacred knowledge? If so what was it? Are they indicating that the Earth will shortly take a sharp deviation from its normal orbital path? What would be the consequences of such a deviation? The next two chapters will look at this scenario.

CH 6

Wisdom of the Ancients

What does all this mean? What were the ancient Egyptians trying to communicate to us?

The Egyptians sometimes spoke of the 'Return of Osiris'. The Christian equivalent would be the Second Coming of Jesus Christ which would inaugurate His Millennial reign.

Is the rising of Orion to its zenith with its raised limb on the ecliptic one of the signs of the times? As Orion = Osiris = Christ, is it a sign of the Son of Man in Heaven? Is it a harbinger of the disruption of the Sun and Earth's motions and of the imminent destruction facing many of mankind? In Matthew 24:35 we read 'But of that day and hour knoweth no man, no, not the angels of heaven, but my Father only.' However, although we do not know the day or the hour, do we have an indicator of the likely decade or so in which these things will occur?

Interestingly, the constellation of Draco,—The Dragon, has been descending whilst Orion has been ascending and Draco is now at its lowest point (with its head over the UK bowing to modern Israel!) in the sky. It will remain there for approximately a thousand years. The Dragon is traditionally another name for the Devil and we think of the scripture in Doctrine & Covenants 88:110 (Smith, Doctrine and Covenants, 1844)—

'And so on, until the seventh angel shall sound his trump; and he shall stand forth upon the land and upon the sea, and swear in the name of him who sitteth upon the throne, that there shall be time no longer; and Satan shall be bound, that old serpent, who is called the devil, and shall not be loosed for the space of a thousand years'.

Also in Revelations 20:2

'And he laid hold on the dragon, that old serpent, which is the Devil, and Satan, and bound him a thousand years',

Indeed the dragon will be bound both actually and astrologically!

CH 7

An Orbital Deviation

If the current position of the Orion constellation indicates a deviation in the ecliptic is imminent, we might ask ourselves what would be the effect of a deviation in the Earth's path? The effect of such sudden change in the Earth's motion could be catastrophic for its inhabitants. Any sudden change in the Earth's movement or rotation, for example, would result in huge tsunamis sweeping the globe on a scale unknown in the modern era of man. If the rotation of the Earth slowed down, the seas would recede to the poles and if the Earth's rotation speeded up the opposite would occur. Global earthquakes would occur because of the forces on the Earth's crust and vulcanism on an apocalyptic scale would be unleashed. The skies would darken because of all the dust and ash that would be spewed out by the volcanoes and the sun and moon would be reddened and difficult to see. Thus the sun 'will refuse to give its light' i.e. be darkened and the moon 'will be 'turned to blood' i.e. it will appear dark red in colour.

Does this seem fanciful? Well it isn't because it exactly matches the upheavals foretold in the scriptures! Let us first look at Revelation 6:12-17

> 12 And I beheld when he had opened the sixth seal, and, lo, there was a great earthquake; and the sun became black as sackcloth of hair, and the moon became as blood;
> 13 And the stars of heaven fell unto the earth, even as a fig tree casteth her untimely figs, when she is shaken of a mighty wind.

31

14 And the heaven departed as a scroll when it is rolled together; and every mountain and island were moved out of their places.

15 And the kings of the earth, and the great men, and the rich men, and the chief captains, and the mighty men, and every bondman, and every free man, hid themselves in the dens and in the rocks of the mountains;

16 And said to the mountains and rocks, Fall on us, and hide us from the face of him that sitteth on the throne, and from the wrath of the Lamb:

17 For the great day of his wrath is come; and who shall be able to stand?

And also at Revelation 16:17, 18

17 And the seventh angel poured out his vial into the air; and there came a great voice out of the temple of heaven, from the throne, saying, It is done.

18 And there were voices, and thunders, and lightnings; and there was a great earthquake, such as was not since men were upon the earth, so mighty an earthquake, and so great.

So an earthquake larger than any that have so far occurred while man has been on the Earth is going to happen. It will cause the effects we have discussed above and will re-order the land masses of the Earth so that they return as they were 'in the days of Peleg' i.e. all will become one landmass. The kingdoms of the Earth will perish and their kings and mighty men will hide themselves in crevices in the rocks for fear of the Lord. The Lord has warned us in modern scripture of great tribulations prior to the second coming of Christ. If we look at D&C 49:23 (Smith, Doctrine and Covenants, 1844), we read:

Wherefore, be not deceived, but continue in steadfastness, looking forth for the heavens to be shaken, and the earth to tremble and to reel to and fro as a drunken man, and for the valleys to be exalted, and for the mountains to be made low, and for the rough places to become smooth—and all this when the angel shall sound his trumpet.

Figure 17—New York—Will this Great Metropolis be Destroyed?

Similarly, in D&C 88:87 (Smith, Doctrine and Covenants, 1844) we read:

> 'For not many days hence and the earth shall tremble and reel to and fro as a drunken man; and the sun shall hide his face, and shall refuse to give light; and the moon shall be bathed in blood; and the stars shall become exceedingly angry, and shall cast themselves down as a fig that falleth from off a fig tree'.

Many of us will have seen a child's spinning top wobbling after it has been pushed by a lateral force. It reels to and fro 'like a drunken man' as its axis precesses wildly. Presumably, therefore, the Earth will be subject to a lateral force which will cause its axis to precess more than usual and the Earth will appear to 'wobble' in space. Again, the motion will not be so violent as to kill all humankind but its effects will certainly kill many.

Figure 18—Las Vegas—Will this be Among the Cities to be Destroyed?

The great cities of the Earth such as New York, London, Paris, Las Vegas etc will be destroyed by the convulsions of nature and law and order will break down. Great dams will be ruptured and flood enormous tracts of land and essential services such as water, gas, and electricity will cease functioning. Governments will lose control, financial institutions and companies will cease to exist and the Earth will become a home to bandits and desperate men. They will roam the Earth looking for food and will stop at nothing to get it.

If we look at D&C 133: 23-24; (Smith, Doctrine and Covenants, 1844) we can read:

> 'He shall command the great deep, and it shall be driven back into the north countries, and the islands shall become one land; And the land of Jerusalem and the land of Zion shall be turned back into their own place, and the earth shall be like as it was in the days before it was divided.' Thus it appears that the Earth's speed of rotation will be slowed down as the waters

are described as receding to the North. It will have to be only a slight reduction in speed of rotation or the effects would be too catastrophic for any humans to survive!

Figure 19—The Hoover Dam—Will this Great Dam be Ruptured?

The oceans will be banished to the poles and the lands of the Earth will be joined together as they were prior to the days of Peleg in the Old Testament. (see Genesis 10:25)

Meanwhile, the Lord will call his faithful to gather in appointed places and they will begin to build the New Jerusalem and Temple in Independence, Missouri and the Old Jerusalem with a new Temple in Israel.

Figure 20—Jerusalem Showing The Dome of the Rock on the Temple Site

CH 8

THE SATURN MYTH

Interestingly, other theories, books and ideas point to the Earth's motion and configuration being changed prior to the second coming. In 'The Saturn Myth' (Talbot, 1980), we read of a golden age in the past when the Earth was a much more pleasant place to live than it is today. This was a time when the Earth was in a terrestrial state like Eden rather than its current telestial state. At that time Saturn hovered over the North pole bestowing all manner of benefits on the Earth. Its axis of rotation was aligned with that of the Earth. Jupiter and other planets may have also been in the alignment. There is much evidence in myths pointing to such a planetary configuration. These myths are referred to in 'Hamlet's Mill' (Dechend, 1969) by Santillana and Von Dechend.

Early Sumero-Babylonian texts call Saturn the 'Sun Star'. The Babylonian sun god was Shamash and scholars largely equate this God with our present Sun. However, anciently the Sumero-Babylonians stated unequivocally that 'the planet Saturn is Shamash'. Thus they equated Saturn with their concept of the sun. Talbot indicates that this is evidence that Saturn in ancient times was much nearer to the Earth and more prominent than the sun is now. So much so that there was a flux tube joining the two spheres through which they interchanged water and other materials which benefited conditions on the Earth. For many ancient civilizations, the day began at the setting of the solar orb. This was because Saturn was the great god of the day who gave light throughout what we now call night. Presumably this reflected or secondary light from Saturn was not as harmful as direct sunlight is to us. This and other beneficial effects of the planetary configuration could be some of the reasons that the patriarchs of the Old Testament lived to such ripe old ages.

The 'dumbbell' configuration of planets implied by the above theory has incurred much criticism from physicists and astronomers but others have proposed various ingenious scientific solutions to what seems initially to be an impossible planetary configuration. Frederick B Jueneman (Jueneman, 1975) proposed what he called a 'barbell' configuration in which two planets would orbit the sun together with their poles facing each other revolving about a common axis. In addition, each planet would describe a secondary orbit around the axis of a cone. The gravitational centre of this system would be where the two cones meet.

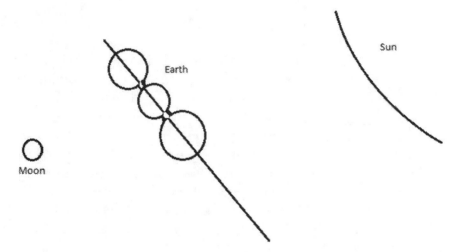

Figure 21—Representation of Sketch of Ancient Earth by Joseph Smith

It is very interesting, in this context, that there is a diagram of the Earth's ancient appearance ascribed to Joseph Smith (Brough, 1979). It is claimed that this diagram was sketched around 1842 by the prophet and kept by Philo Dibble an early LDS member. It was passed down to Sydney Dibble, Philo's son and was along the lines of figure 21. The other spheres attached to the Earth could be Saturn and or Jupiter etc. Presumably the lost tribes or the city of Enoch could have migrated away from the Earth on such a sphere if it became detached from the Earth.

One might speculate on whether the change from a terrestrial state to a telestial state on Earth came about after the fall and banishment from the Garden of Eden or whether it occurred at the flood of Noah. Certainly we are given to understand that there was no rain on Earth prior to the flood of Noah and that the Earth was watered by a heavy overnight dew. Some have speculated that Noah's flood was triggered by the waters which were previously held at the pole by Saturn being released as Saturn moved away from the Earth.

In the third book of his trilogy, 'And there shall be a New Heaven and a New Earth' (Larson, 1985) Larson develops this theme and implies that the Earth will return to this terrestrial barbell state during the millennium after an upheaval prior to the second coming of the Saviour. Any such upheaval involving the alteration of planetary orbits including that of the Earth is certain to have tragic consequences for most of those living on the Earth at that time.

In the Kolob Theorem (Hilton, 2006) Hilton proposes that, at the start of the millennium, the Earth will be moved to the terrestrial zone of the Milky Way galaxy from its current telestial zone. Whether the Sun or other planets in the solar system will go with it is not specified but clearly a great disruption of the Earth's current motion is envisaged.

All these theories have one thing in common with the view of the ancient Egyptians viz. the motion of the Earth will be violently disrupted prior to the start of the millennium.

Now let us look at some other interesting developments that also suggest that the second coming of Jesus Christ is fast approaching.

CH 9

THE SHEPHERD STONE OF ISRAEL

In Gen 28 we read how, on his way to Padan-Aram, Jacob stopped to sleep at Luz in the desert. Whilst there, he chose a stone which he used as a pillow. The stone had been prepared for use as part of a holy building but had been rejected by the masons because it had a flaw in it. It was a suitable shape to be used as a pillow. Verse 18 continues:

> 'And Jacob rose up early in the morning, and took the stone that he had put for his pillows, and set it up for a pillar, and poured oil upon the top of it'.

So we see that there Jacob anointed the stone and in subsequent verses he covenanted to tithe his increase and he renamed the place Beth-El meaning House of God. Jacob was renamed Israel and begat the twelve sons that became the twelve tribes of Israel. The pillar stone of Jacob (Israel) became sacred to the twelve tribes of Israel. They called it the 'Shepherd Stone'. Iron rings were set in each end and the Israelites carried it with them on their travels by inserting poles through the rings and placing the poles on the shoulders of the bearers. They took it to Egypt with them during the famine when Joseph rescued and fed them. Later they took it with them as they left Egypt with Moses.

In Gen 49:22-26 we can read how Jacob blessed Joseph and mentioned the stone 'from thence is the shepherd the stone of Israel?' Walker (Walker, 1999) suggested that this should read 'from thence is the Shepherd Stone of Israel?' This implies that Joseph and his birthright son Ephraim and their descendants will be the possessors of the Shepherd Stone of Israel. (This statement does not refer to Christ since he is of the line of Judah).

Figure 22—The Shepherd Stone or Stone of Destiny

The stone was placed in Solomon's Temple and all the Kings of Israel of the House of David were crowned sitting on it or standing by it e. g. 2 Kings ll: l2-l4. This is the only stone in the Bible that was anointed and it represents Christ - 'The Shepherd of Israel'. The stone which the original Temple builders rejected became the Head or Coronation Stone on which the Kings of Israel were crowned. Similarly, Christ was rejected (see Psalms 118:22) but will become the headstone of the corner—King of All.

At the beginning of the 6th century BC, the Babylonians besieged Jerusalem and took it and sacked it. The King of Judah, Zedekiah, was blinded and taken into captivity where he died. His sons (apart from Mulek) were killed in his sight before he was blinded. Two of his daughters, however, escaped in the care of Jeremiah and his scribe Baruch and went to Egypt (Jer 43:7-8). Jeremiah was told that he and his party would be looked after in difficult times and that he would go to a land which he knew not. (see Jer 15:11-14 Also Isaiah 37:31-32). There the House of Judah would again grow and prosper.

Anthony W Ivins (Ivins) who was an Apostle and counsellor to Heber J Grant said:

> 'After the conquest of Palestine, the Babylonian armies invaded Egypt and it became evident that they would be victorious over the Egyptians. Just at this time we lose sight of Jeremiah and these two girls, so far as the Bible is concerned. Just at that time a ship landed on the coast of Spain, from which an old man and his secretary and two young women disembarked. They remained for a short while in that country, where one of the girls married into the reigning house of Spain, but the old man, who is referred to in Ireland as Ollamh Fodhla (pro Feehola) or the old prophet, in their traditions and songs which they still sing of him, passed across the channel and landed on the coast of Ireland taking with him the elder of the two girls, whose name was Tamar Tephi, which translated from Hebrew to English means beautiful Palm; or the beautiful wanderer.'

The old Irish records 'The Chronicles of Eri' (O'Connor, 1822) inform us of the arrival of an old prophet and a princess in Ireland and give a date of 582/3 BC. They brought with them David's harp and a stone which the Irish called Lia-Fail meaning 'Stone of Destiny'. According to Milner, (Milner, 1991) the old prophet or 'Ollam Fola' as he was called was surely Jeremiah who had a mission to build and plant. Tamar Tephi, the princess, was surely Zedekiah's daughter seeking a husband of the royal line of Judah. The Stone of Destiny was the Shepherd Stone of Israel. Totten's 'Old Irish Genealogies' confirms that all ancient Irish Kings were crowned on the 'Lia-Fail' or 'Stone of Destiny' for a period of 1083 years.

The princess, daughter of Zedekiah of the Pharez line of Judah, later married 'Eochaidh the Heremon', the King of Ireland who was descended from the Zarah line of Judah. This re-united the two lines of Judah that had separated acrimoniously in Egypt. The Stone of Destiny was later taken to Scotland by Fergus MacErc V when he succeeded in taking possession of Argyll in the 5th century AD. Later it was moved to Scone by Kenneth MacAlpin, the 36th King of Dalriada. It was placed upon the

Moot Hill and used in the coronations of the Kings of Scots until the end of the 13th century. Lulach—stepson of Macbeth—sat on it when he was proclaimed King of Scots in 1057.

Later in 995AD, King Kenneth II of Scotland had inscribed on the stone:

> 'If fate go right, where'er this Stone be found,
> The Scots shall monarchs of that realm be found.'

When, in 1296AD, Edward I of England removed the stone to Westminster Abbey, London it appeared that the inscription would not be fulfilled. Edward placed the stone in a compartment under the seat of a chair he had made. The special chair was called St Edward's Chair or the Coronation Chair. Ever since Edward, all Kings and Queens of England have been crowned on it (the only exceptions being Edward V and Edward VIII.). But the inscription became once more true when James VI of Scotland was invited to become James I of the United Kingdom of England and Scotland (1603AD) under the Union of James flag (the Union Jack).

Ezekiel, a contemporary of Jeremiah, predicted three overturns or moves of the Stone of Destiny and the accompanying throne of the line of Judah. In Ezek 21:25-27, Zedekiah was the wicked prince spoken of and the 1st overthrow was from Zedekiah King of Judah to Ireland via Zedekiah's daughter. The 2nd overthrow was from the Irish Tara Kings to Scotland via Fergus MacErc in Argyll. The 3rd overthrow was from the Scottish Jacobite Kings to England via Edward I and James I. Some believed that the scripture indicated that the Stone of Destiny would remain in Westminster Abbey until second coming of Jesus Christ (He who comes Whose right it is to reign). However, a possible interpretation of the scripture is that the Stone of Destiny might be moved again when the Saviour's return is imminent, in preparation for that event. In 1950, four students removed the Stone from Westminster Abbey in London. It soon turned up at Arbroath Abbey, north-east of Edinburgh. The abbey is famous for the Declaration of Arbroath, a robust statement of Scotland's independence from England. The stone was returned to Westminster Abbey.

Now the Stone of Destiny has recently been moved again back to Scotland! In 1996, Her Majesty The Queen allowed the stone to be returned to Scotland, after 700 years. It is now housed in Edinburgh Castle.

This is an indication that the second coming is imminent and that the Saviour has some reason for wanting the stone in Edinburgh at his coming. Is it because much of London is quite low lying and will be inundated in the upheavals of nature which precede the Second Coming? It implies that no more British monarchs will be crowned before Christ comes again (unless they travel to Edinburgh for coronation or borrow the stone back again). As the current monarch is quite elderly, this suggests that the second coming of Christ cannot be far away.

CH 10

America to Become a Great Nation

The discovery of the Americas and in particular the USA was foretold in scripture. 1ˢᵗ Nephi 13:12-16 refers. (Smith, The Book of Mormon, 1830)

> 12 And I looked and beheld a man *[Columbus]* among the Gentiles, who was separated from the seed of my brethren *[Indians]* by the many waters; and I beheld the Spirit of God, that it came down and wrought upon the man; and he went forth upon the many waters, even unto the seed of my brethren, who were in the promised land.
>
> 13 And it came to pass that I beheld the Spirit of God, that it wrought upon other Gentiles; and they went forth out of captivity, upon the many waters.
>
> 14 And it came to pass that I beheld many multitudes of the Gentiles upon the land of promise; and I beheld the wrath of God, that it was upon the seed of my brethren; and they were scattered before the Gentiles and were smitten.
>
> 15 And I beheld the Spirit of the Lord, that it was upon the Gentiles *[colonists]*, and they did prosper and obtain the land for their inheritance; and I beheld that they were white, and exceedingly fair and beautiful, like unto my people before they were slain.
>
> 16 And it came to pass that I, Nephi, beheld that the Gentiles who had gone forth out of captivity did humble

themselves before the Lord; and the power of the Lord was with them.

Those who colonised the original thirteen states of the USA eventually prospered. Many of them fled there from Europe for religious freedom. Nephi continues the story in 1ˢᵗ Nephi 13:17-19 (Smith, The Book of Mormon, 1830)

> 17 And I beheld that their mother Gentiles [*Great Britain*] were gathered together upon the waters, and upon the land also, to battle against them.
> 18 And I beheld that the power of God was with them, and also that the wrath of God was upon all those that were gathered together against them to battle.
> 19 And I, Nephi, beheld that the Gentiles that had gone out of captivity were delivered by the power of God out of the hands of all other nations.

Thus we see that the original thirteen states were delivered by the hand of the Lord from what was then the most powerful nation on Earth (Great Britain). We note further from the Book of Mormon that it was prophesied long ago that the Lord would raise up a mighty nation on the American continent. 1 Nephi 22:7 (Smith, The Book of Mormon, 1830)

> 7 And it meaneth that the time cometh that after all the house of Israel have been scattered and confounded, that the Lord God will raise up a mighty nation among the Gentiles, yea, even upon the face of this land; and by them shall our seed be scattered.

This has come to pass as prophesied and since the time of the first world war, the USA has gradually risen to become the pre-eminent nation on the Earth, eclipsing all others in wealth and power. The USA is also the bread basket of the world producing huge amounts of grain and food, some of which it donates to poor nations.

When looking to the last days, it was prophesied by Joseph Smith that the time would come when the constitution of the United States would be on the brink of ruin and that the Church and its members would be the ones to save it from such a fate.

"Even this nation will be on the verge of crumbling to pieces and tumbling to the ground and when the Constitution is on the brink of ruin this people will be the staff upon which the nation shall lean and they shall bear the Constitution away from the very verge of destruction." (Smith, Joseph Smith Papers, 1844).)

The prophet Brigham Young also had something to say about this situation. Journal of Discourses Vol 2 p182. (Various, Journal of Discourses Vol 2, 1855)

"When the Constitution of the United States hangs, as it were, upon a single thread, they will have to call for the 'Mormon' elders to save it from utter destruction; and they will step forth and do it."

Even more recent were the comments of Prophet Ezra Taft Benson when he said: (Benson, 1987)

"Unfortunately, we as a nation have apostatized in various degrees from different Constitutional principles as proclaimed by the inspired founders. We are fast approaching that moment prophesied by Joseph Smith when he said: 'Even this nation will be on the verge of crumbling to pieces and tumbling to the ground and when the Constitution is on the brink of ruin this people will be the staff upon which the nation shall lean and they shall bear the Constitution away from the very verge of destruction.'"

Clearly we are approaching a time when the Constitution will be threatened. Looking at the political situation today, some Church members who are politicians are becoming increasingly influential in the US. All Utah's senators are Mormons and one of them is Senate Majority Leader Harry Reid, the most powerful man in the US upper house. Another, Orrin Hatch, is one of the country's most senior opposition leaders. Even more recently, Mitt Romney has become the Republican frontrunner to challenge Barrack Obama at the next election. It is conceivable that there will be a Mormon President! Will this enable the Church and its people to rescue the constitution when it is under threat in some way?

The Constitution of the United States was divinely inspired. It is referred to in the Doctrine and Covenants 101:77-80 (Smith, Doctrine and Covenants, 1844)

77 According to the laws and constitution of the people, which I have suffered to be established, and should be maintained for the rights and protection of all flesh, according to just and holy principles;

78 That every man may act in doctrine and principle pertaining to futurity, according to the moral agency which I have given unto him, that every man may be accountable for his own sins in the day of judgment.

79 Therefore, it is not right that any man should be in bondage one to another.

80 And for this purpose have I established the Constitution of this land, by the hands of wise men whom I raised up unto this very purpose, and redeemed the land by the shedding of blood.

We see that one of the purposes of the Constitution was to maintain the rights of all men according to just and holy principles. Recent court decisions have begun to interpret the Constitution in ways that God would not approve. Religious freedoms, laws and rights are being subordinated to modern equality and discrimination laws. It might be that one way in which the Church will assist to protect the Constitution will be in driving the interpretation of it in a righteous direction. This was implied by George Q Cannon when he said: (p104) (Various, Journal of Discourses Vol 23, 1881)

"The day will come—and this is another prediction of Joseph Smith's—I want to remind you of it, my brethren and sisters, when good government, constitutional government—liberty will be found among the Latter-day Saints, and it will be sought for in vain elsewhere, when the Constitution of this land and republican government and institutions will be upheld by this people who are now so oppressed and whose destruction is now sought so diligently. The day will come when the Constitution, and free government under it, will be sustained and preserved by this people."

That day is fast approaching.

CH 11

THE TEMPLE AT JERUSALEM

Many will be unaware that there is a group of faithful Jews ('The Temple Institute') who have been preparing and making items for a third Temple at Jerusalem. They have painstakingly researched original designs, materials and construction methods in order to reproduce the original Temple vessels and artefacts as closely as possible. Items known to have been produced so far are:-

Golden Menorah
Brass Laver
High Priest's Crown (Tsitz)
High Priest's Breastplate
Priest's and High Priest's Robes and Sash
Uncut Stones for an Altar
The Golden Lamp of Queen Helena

All these items can be viewed on the internet at:
http://www.templeinstitute.org/vessels_gallery_11.htm

These people are lobbying the Israeli Parliament to be allowed to rebuild the Temple in Jerusalem into which these precious items would be placed. Priestly Levites of the Cohen line have been identified and trained in Temple ordinances and sacrifices.

There are also some Jews breeding a pure red heifer from which to originate purifying ash/water (see Ch 12). The latest news is that they have successfully bred a kosher red heifer.

Jewish historians have sought to establish the exact site of the original Temples of Solomon and Zerubbabel in which the ancient Jews and Israel worshipped. There are those who assume they were built round the rock on the top of Mount Moriah. As this site is now occupied by the Muslim Dome of the Rock sanctuary, this causes friction with adherents of the Muslim religion. However, the Temple Mount area is huge and there is ample room for a Jewish Temple on the Mount without it impinging upon the Dome of the Rock or the Al-Aqsa mosque. Indeed some prominent Jewish historians have made strong cases that the original Temples were built either North of the Dome of the Rock sanctuary or South of it. Thus the new third Temple could be built on the original Temple site without affecting the Muslim sanctuaries. Recently, faithful Jews looking to the rebuilding of the Temple produced some architectural drawings for aspects of the outer courts of the Temple. If some change of circumstances makes it possible to rebuild the Temple at Jerusalem on the original Temple Mount, it would be done quickly.

The Church of Jesus Christ of Latter Day Saints maintains an educational centre on Mount Scopus near the Mount of Olives. The centre houses study abroad programs of Brigham Young University and also occasional concerts and conferences. It is not designed to ever be converted into a Temple. It is however, a spectacular building with attractive architecture and gardens which overlook the Old City of Jerusalem. An introductory video is available on the internet which gives a good view of the facilities of the centre.

The Mount of Olives is the place where, according to prophecy, Christ will appear in glory at his second coming. The Mount will cleave in two at his presence and Christ will rescue the Jews from their enemies. Zechariah 14:4 refers.

> 4 ¶And his feet shall stand in that day upon the mount of
> Olives, which *is* before Jerusalem on the east, and the mount
> of Olives shall cleave in the midst thereof toward the east and
> toward the west, *and there shall be* a very great valley; and half

of the mountain shall remove toward the north, and half of it
toward the south.

Some Christians say the Temple at Jerusalem will be built after the
Messiah returns in glory but many believe it will happen before He comes.
Joseph Smith was in the latter category and he stated:

"Judah must return, Jerusalem must be rebuilt, and the temple, and
water come out from under the temple, and the waters of the Dead Sea
be healed. It will take some time to rebuild the walls of the city and the
temple, . . . and all this must be done before the Son of Man will make His
appearance" (Smith, Teachings of the Prophet Joseph Smith, 1976)

We learn from this that the third Temple will be built by the Jews
before the Saviour returns in glory and that water will flow out from under
the Temple and heal the Dead Sea. Ezekiel has much to say on this subject
and we will quote him in full.

Ezekiel 47:1-10

> 1 Afterward he brought me again unto the door of the
> house; and, behold, waters issued out from under the threshold
> of the house eastward: for the forefront of the house *stood*
> *toward* the east, and the waters came down from under from
> the right side of the house, at the south *side* of the altar.
>
> 2 Then brought he me out of the way of the gate northward,
> and led me about the way without unto the utter gate by the
> way that looketh eastward; and, behold, there ran out waters
> on the right side.
>
> 3 And when the man that had the line in his hand went
> forth eastward, he measured a thousand cubits, and he brought
> me through the waters; the waters *were* to the ankles.
>
> 4 Again he measured a thousand, and brought me through
> the waters; the waters *were* to the knees. Again he measured
> a thousand, and brought me through; the waters *were* to the
> loins.
>
> 5 Afterward he measured a thousand; *and it was* a river
> that I could not pass over: for the waters were risen, waters to
> swim in, a river that could not be passed over.

6 ¶And he said unto me, Son of man, hast thou seen *this?* Then he brought me, and caused me to return to the brink of the river.

7 Now when I had returned, behold, at the bank of the river *were* very many trees on the one side and on the other.

8 Then said he unto me, These waters issue out toward the east country, and go down into the desert, and go into the sea: *which being* brought forth into the sea, the waters shall be healed.

9 And it shall come to pass, *that* every thing that liveth, which moveth, whithersoever the rivers shall come, shall live: and there shall be a very great multitude of fish, because these waters shall come thither: for they shall be healed; and every thing shall live whither the river cometh.

10 And it shall come to pass, *that* the fishers shall stand upon it from En-gedi even unto En-eglaim; they shall be a *place* to spread forth nets; their fish shall be according to their kinds, as the fish of the great sea, exceeding many.

Thus we see that Joseph Smith was referring to Ezekiel's prophesy that water must flow out from under the Temple at Jerusalem at the second coming of the Saviour. This is further evidence of movements in the Earth's crust prior to the Millennium. The water which flows out from under the Temple will form a river which, according to Joseph Smith will flow into the Dead Sea and revitalise it. It is possible that this will occur as the Saviour descends onto the Mount of Olives and causes it to split in two leaving a valley through to the East through which the water can flow to the Dead Sea. The flow will form a substantial river and will increase the amount of fresh water flowing into the Dead Sea considerably. It is possible that the splitting asunder of the Mount of Olives will be part of a larger Earth movement in which the rift valley in which the Dead Sea lies will widen and sink at its Southern end where it meets the Gulf of Aqaba. Thus the way will open for a river to flow out of the Dead Sea and down into the Gulf of Aqaba. This will cause the Dead Sea to quickly become a freshwater lake with a river running out of it to the sea at the Gulf of Aqaba.

The two places En-Gedi and En-Eglaim mentioned by Ezekiel are natural springs thought to be on opposite sides of the Dead Sea. The springs of En-Gedi are substantial year round springs which form an oasis in the desert near the Dead Sea which David of old used as a hiding place when he was fleeing from Saul. Some of the Judean plateau contains limestone and similar rocks which are prone to underground water seepage. The fact that substantial springs such as En-Gedi occur in the Judean hills perhaps indicates that it is not impossible or implausible for a spring to come out from under the Temple Mount.

Latter Day Saints believe that the Sons of Levi must offer again an offering in righteousness to complete the restoration of all things in this the last dispensation of time. This is implied in Doctrine and Covenants 13:1 (Smith, Doctrine and Covenants, 1844)

'Upon you my fellow servants, in the name of Messiah I confer the Priesthood of Aaron, which holds the keys of the ministering of angels, and of the gospel of repentance, and of baptism by immersion for the remission of sins; and this shall never be taken again from the earth, until the sons of Levi do offer again an offering unto the Lord in righteousness'.

This statement was made by John the Baptist as he ordained Joseph Smith and Oliver Cowdery to the Aaronic Priesthood in 1829. One presumes that the offering referred to must be a sacrificial offering such as the Jews have not offered since the destruction of the second Temple in AD 70 by the Romans under Titus. So ordinances will be performed in the third Jerusalem Temple but they may be ordinances of the Aaronic Priesthood.

Also relevant to this subject is 3 Nephi Ch 24 v 1-4 (Smith, The Book of Mormon, 1830)

'Thus said the Father unto Malachi—Behold, I will send my messenger, and he shall prepare the way before me, and the Lord whom ye seek shall suddenly come to his temple, even the messenger of the covenant, whom ye delight in; behold, he shall come, saith the Lord of Hosts.

2 But who may abide the day of his coming, and who shall stand when he appeareth? For he is like a refiner's fire, and like fuller's soap.

3 And he shall sit as a refiner and purifier of silver; and he shall purify the sons of Levi, and purge them as gold and silver, that they may offer unto the Lord an offering in righteousness.

4 Then shall the offering of Judah and Jerusalem be pleasant unto the Lord, as in the days of old, and as in former years.'

This implies that there will be a Temple in Jerusalem to which the Lord will come and purify the Sons of Levi that they may offer an offering in righteousness.

In recent times there have been those who wanted to be able to sacrifice a Paschal lamb on the Temple mount in Jerusalem. This was not allowed under the rules of the Moslem WAQF who govern the mount but might eventually occur in the new Temple.

CH 12

THE TENTH RED HEIFER

What does a red heifer have to do with any of this? It might seem to many to be a complete irrelevance, but to the Jews, the fate of the entire world depends on the red heifer. For its ashes are the essential ingredients for the re-creation of Biblical purity. This, to Jews, is essential for those who are to officiate in the Holy Temple. The ashes of the red heifer have the inexplicable power to cleanse all those who have been rendered unclean

The heifer to be used must be three years old and completely red. This means that there must be no hairs of any other colour and its hooves must be red. It must also be totally free from any physical blemish or defect.

In Jewish law, impurity can be caused by a variety of factors. A common cause is exposure to death or with sickness. Impurity is opposite to the state of holiness and thus one who is impure is forbidden contact with anything holy. He cannot eat of that which is sanctified; neither can he touch that which is holy. He cannot enter a sanctified area and for this reason an individual who has been exposed to death is forbidden to enter the sanctified area of the Temple Mount until he undergoes the process of purification i.e. sprinkling by water with the ashes of the red heifer

The rare event of burning a new heifer for its ashes was an important occasion for the Jews. Because of this, special precautions were taken during the process of the heifer's preparation. They took great care to ensure that the priest was shielded from impurity. The water used came historically from the Pool of Siloam, at the foot of the Temple. This spring was Jerusalem's original source of water and was considered to be holy.

A special bridge was built which led from the eastern gate of the Holy Temple to the spot on the Mount of Olives, where the burning of the heifer was conducted. The heifer and all those who would be aiding or assisting in the ceremony crossed over this bridge to the appointed location on the Mount of Olives.

There was a special mikveh built at this spot for the priest to immerse himself in before starting the ceremony. With their hands upon his head, the elders declared to the High Priest: "Immerse yourself once!" The priest descended into the mikveh and purified himself, and came up and dried himself. Wood was arranged on the altar (cedar, pine, cypress and fig). The fire was lit from its western side, the end facing the Temple. The red heifer was bound to the altar with cords made from reed-grass, which do not become impure. It was placed on top of the pile of wood.

The priest stood atop the altar and slaughtered the heifer. He used his right hand for this act, and then gathered the blood in his left hand. With his right index finger he sprinkled from it seven times, standing opposite the entrance to the Holy Temple. He then left the altar and lit the fire. Cedar wood, hyssop, and wool dyed with scarlet were thrown onto the fire.

After the fire was finished and all had been completely burned, everything there was ground to a powder, and these were the ashes which were saved and used for purity. The ashes would be divided into three portions. One share was placed in the Holy Temple, another portion was kept at the burning place on the Mount of Anointment and the third was divided for use between all the priestly shifts serving in the Temple. The attending priests would then use their portions to purify the ordinary Temple patrons and the impure, while the allotment that was on the mount was to be used for the priest who came to burn a new heifer.

The third portion was kept within the wall in the Holy Temple purely as a remembrance as commanded.

Anyone who has had contact with the dead is impure for seven days. During the course of those days, on the third day and on the seventh day, the individual would be sprinkled with the waters of purification, as follows:

A vessel was filled with water flowing from the spring at the Pool of Siloam. Some of the ashes of the heifer are flung into this same vessel, and this mixture of ashes and water are sprinkled on the body of the man on his third and seventh day, after sunrise. This was done using a bundle of three stalks of hyssop with buds. The tops of the buds are dipped into the solution in the vessel. The hyssop is then used to sprinkle the water onto the person being purified.

Even if a new red heifer could somehow be obtained, slaughtered and burned, how can ritual purity be reinstated without the container of original ashes dating back from the time of Moses? Many people seem to be under the impression that without those original ashes, it would be impossible to purify someone since they would have to mixed in with the new ones, as was done in the past, whenever a red heifer was prepared.

However, the Jews could raise a new red heifer, prepare it in the prescribed manner and raise children in purity to carry out the procedure—even without the original ashes. A perfect heifer, thus born, would be fit to be used for the Temple. That is what is now being done.

From the time of Moses to the end of the Second Temple period there were only nine Red Heifers.

The Mishna teaches that up until the destruction of the Second Temple, ashes had been prepared from a total of only nine red heifers. The very first red heifer was processed by Moses himself—as Numbers Ch 19 states, ". . . that they bring you a red heifer." The second was done by the prophet Ezra in the days of the First Temple, and during the entire era of the Second Temple only seven more heifers were used for ashes. This was enough to provide for the nation's needs for purification throughout all those years.

The names of all the High Priests who prepared those seven heifers during Second Temple times are recorded by the Mishna as follows:

> Simon the Just 2
> Yochanan 2
> Elioenai ben HaQayaph 1
> Chanamel HaMitzri 1
> Yishmael ben Pi'avi 1

Thus, from the time that Moses received the commandment of the red heifer from the Lord, until the destruction of the Second Temple, purifying ashes had been produced by the hands of these great leaders from a total of nine red heifers.

In the Mishna, the great Maimonides gives his opinion that the Tenth Red Heifer will be prepared by the Messiah. Thus Maimonides recounts an ancient tradition—that the tenth red heifer is associated with the Messianic era. However, other Jews believe that the tenth red heifer will be prepared by children raised in purity ready for the coming of the Messiah. Either way, the appearance of a red heifer in these waning end times is an indication, a forerunner of the appearance of the Messiah himself.

The fact that there has been no red heifer for the past 2,000 years perhaps indicates that Israel was not ready. But now, with kosher red heifers being identified, the means for purification is close at hand. With the opinion of Maimonides in mind, we cannot help but speculate that if there are now red heifers being raised, then is this the era in which the Jews will need them to purify those who will offer an offering in righteousness?

CH 13

Modern Jerusalem

The scriptures prophesy that modern Israel and Jerusalem will become an obstacle and a burdensome threat to all those who would fight against it.

Zechariah 12:2, 3

> 2 Behold, I will make Jerusalem a cup of trembling unto all the people round about, when they shall be in the siege both against Judah *and* against Jerusalem.
>
> 3 ¶And in that day will I make Jerusalem a burdensome stone for all people: all that burden themselves with it shall be cut in pieces, though all the people of the earth be gathered together against it.

We already know that the nations which surround Israel are generally not pro Israel. Indeed they fought against Israel in 1967 when, as foretold in the scriptures, Israel won the war against a numerically much larger force. In that war Israel took control of Jerusalem and the West Bank territories from Jordan. Also, Gaza and the Golan heights were taken from Egypt and Syria respectively. Israel has built a reputation for striking back quickly and effectively against all those who attack it or practise terrorism inside its boundaries. It could be said that most of the nations of the world are involved with Jerusalem in that the United Nations has repeatedly sought a peaceful solution to the problems of the West Bank and Jerusalem and the Palestinian problem. So far they have been unsuccessful in finding a permanent solution, probably because there cannot be a permanent solution until the Saviour comes a second time.

Zechariah 12:8, 9

> 8 In that day shall the LORD defend the inhabitants of Jerusalem; and he that is feeble among them at that day shall be as David; and the house of David *shall be* as God, as the angel of the LORD before them.
>
> 9 And it shall come to pass in that day, *that* I will seek to destroy all the nations that come against Jerusalem.

The Lord will defend the inhabitants of Jerusalem and it will be as David. As we recall from the scriptures, David successfully defeated all the enemies of Israel. He defeated Goliath, which perhaps implies that Israel will be able to defeat larger forces than its own which gather against it. Moreover, the Lord states that He will 'destroy all the nations that come against Jerusalem'. It would seem that those nations which openly state that they wish to destroy Israel and Jerusalem will not succeed, at least until the final conflict of Armageddon (see Ch 14).

Not only will the Lord deliver Israel/Judah from those that held it in captivity, but he will cause those that would seek to oppress Israel/Judah to turn in upon themselves and fight amongst themselves.

Isaiah 49:25, 26

> 25 But thus saith the LORD, Even the captives of the mighty shall be taken away, and the prey of the terrible shall be delivered: for I will contend with him that contendeth with thee, and I will save thy children.
>
> 26 And I will feed them that oppress thee with their own flesh; and they shall be drunken with their own blood, as with sweet wine: and all flesh shall know that I the LORD *am* thy Saviour and thy Redeemer, the mighty One of Jacob.

It is interesting to note that many of the nations round about Israel who have sought to oppress or attack Israel have suffered or are suffering internal turmoil and terrorism which has caused many casualties. Examples of this are the Sunni/Shiite Muslim struggles and the 'Arab Spring' uprisings.

CH 14

ISRAEL AND THE UN

The United Nations (UN), led by the powerful nations of the West, is currently favourable to Israel. Israel has been known in the past to make pre-emptive strikes against belligerent nations which are trying to develop an aggressive or nuclear capability. It could do so again. However, if the day should come that Israel oversteps the mark in defence of its territory, then the UN could put sanctions on Israel. If these prove insufficient to correct the perceived aberrant behaviour, military steps could be taken against Israel thus setting the scene for an Armageddon type conflict scenario.

President Woodruff has also discussed this subject: '. . . O house of Judah, . . . It is true that after you return and gather your nation home, and rebuild your City and Temple, that the Gentiles will gather together their armies to go against you to battle, to take you a prey and to take you as a spoil, which they will do, for the words of your prophets must be fulfilled. . . .' (Cowley, 1964)

Elder Charles W Penrose wrote: 'The bankrupt nations, envying the wealth of the sons of Judah, will seek a pretext to make war on them, and will invade the holy land to take a prey and a spoil'. (Penrose, 1859)

We see already that the once affluent nations of the West are becoming increasingly burdened with debt and close to bankruptcy. Thus the nations of the world, under the guise of the UN, could find a reason to attack Israel, thus triggering an Armageddon type scenario. If this occurs, the surrounding Arab nations would be only too glad to join in and assist the UN!

Let us see what the scriptures have to say about this event. Revelation 16:14-16

> 14 For they are the spirits of devils, working miracles, *which* go forth unto the kings of the earth and of the whole world, to gather them to the battle of that great day of God Almighty.
>
> 15 Behold, I come as a thief. Blessed *is* he that watcheth, and keepeth his garments, lest he walk naked, and they see his shame.
>
> 16 And he gathered them together into a place called in the Hebrew tongue Armageddon.

So the kings and armies of the world will be involved, mostly against Israel but possibly some for Israel. The battle will happen at a place called Armageddon which in modern parlance is the site of the ancient hill city of Megiddo which overlooks the strategic Jezreel valley or Plain of Esdraelon. This was the site of battles in antiquity because the valley leads from the East across to the Mediterranean coast. The Israelites will be overcome and Jerusalem will eventually be besieged. Note the interesting comment about those who keep their garments or covenants. If this battle is after the Earth's motion has been disturbed, it could be a disorganised rabble going up to take a spoil of Jerusalem.

In the eleventh chapter of Revelation, John gives us more detail about the siege of Jerusalem. Parley P Pratt explained it thus: (Pratt P. P., 1837)

"John in his 11th chapter of Revelation, gives us many more particulars concerning this same event. He informs us that, after the city and temple are rebuilt by the Jews, the Gentiles will tread it under foot forty and two months, during which time there will be two Prophets continually prophesying and working mighty miracles. And it seems that the Gentile army shall be hindered from utterly destroying and overthrowing the city, while these two Prophets continue. But, after a struggle of three years and a half, they at length succeed in destroying these two Prophets, and then over-running much of the city, they send gifts to each other because of the death of the two Prophets, and in the meantime will not allow their dead bodies to be put in graves, but suffer them to lie in the streets of Jerusalem three days and a half, during which the armies of the Gentiles, consisting of many kindreds, tongues and nations, passing through the city, plundering the Jews, see their dead bodies lying in the street. But after three days and a half, on a sudden, the spirit of life from God enters them, and they will rise and stand upon their feet, and great fear will fall upon them that see them. And then they shall hear a voice from heaven saying, "Come up hither," and they will ascend up to heaven in a cloud, and their enemies beholding them."

It is at this point that a great earthquake occurs, splitting the Mount of Olives in two as Jesus Christ returns in glory and descends upon the Mount. At the critical point when all seems lost, the Jews will flee through the valley thus created and Christ will rescue them.

CH 15

Adam-ondi-Ahman

In his book The Millennial Messiah, (McConkie, 1982) Bruce R. McConkie gives an excellent opening regarding the mystery of Adam-ondi-Ahman: 'We now come to the least known and least understood thing connected with the Second Coming. It might well be termed the best-kept secret set forth in the revealed word. It is something about which the world knows nothing; it is a doctrine that has scarcely dawned on most of the Latter-day Saints themselves; and yet it is set forth in holy writ and in the teachings of the Prophet Joseph Smith with substantially the same clarity as any of the doctrines of the kingdom'.

By latter-day revelation we know that there was a gathering at Adam-ondi-Ahman, which was attended by all of Adam's righteous posterity and to which the Lord himself came. This occurred three years previous to Adam's death when he called the sons of his lineage (in order: Seth, Enos, Cainan, Mahalaleel, Jared, Enoch, and Methuselah) with the "residue of his posterity who were righteous . . . into the valley of Adam-ondi-Ahman, and there bestowed upon them his last blessing. D&C 107:53-57: (Smith, 1844) refers:

> 'And the Lord appeared unto them, and they rose up and blessed Adam, and called him Michael the Prince, the Archangel.
>
> And the Lord administered comfort unto Adam, and said unto him, I have set thee to be at the head; a multitude of

nations shall come of thee; and thou art a prince over them forever.

And Adam stood up in the midst of the congregation, and notwithstanding he was bowed down with age, being full of the Holy Ghost, predicted whatsoever should befall his posterity unto the latest generation.

These things were all written in the Book of Enoch, and are to be testified of in due time'.

Also in (Smith, Teachings of the Prophet Joseph Smith, 1976):

'I saw Adam in the valley of Adam-ondi-Ahman. He called together his children and blessed them with a patriarchal blessing. The Lord appeared in their midst, and he (Adam) blessed them all, and foretold what should befall them to the latest generation.

"Ahman is one of the names by which God was known to Adam. Ahman is twice mentioned as one of the names of God in the Doctrine and Covenants. The term 'ondi' expresses an ongoing relationship or communication and is probably taken from the Adamaic language. A study of the comments of early brethren who associated with the Prophet Joseph Smith leads to the understanding that 'Adam-ondi-Ahman' means the place or land where Adam communed with God. Orson Pratt interpreted the name to mean 'Valley of God, where Adam dwelt.' (Ludlow, 1991)

The Prophet Joseph Smith taught that "the Garden of Eden was on the American continent located where the City Zion, or the New Jerusalem, will be built. After being expelled from the Garden of Eden, Adam later dwelt in Adam-ondi-Ahman.

Adam built an altar on a hill above the valley of Adam-ondi-Ahman. There the Lord revealed to Adam the purpose of sacrifices and of the fall and the mission of the Saviour

The Doctrine & Covenants tells us that Adam-ondi-Ahman was so named by the Lord "'because, said he, it is the place where Adam shall come to visit his people, or the Ancient of Days shall sit, as spoken of by

Daniel the prophet (D&C 116) (Smith, Doctrine and Covenants, 1844). Hence there will be a gathering or meeting at Adam-ondi-Ahman prior to the second coming of the Saviour at the Mount of Olives. Jesus Christ will be present at that meeting.

Daniel gives us a full description of the gathering which will occur at Adam-ondi-Ahman at the start of the Millenium. Daniel 7:9-14 refers.

> 9 ¶I beheld till the thrones were cast down, and the Ancient of days did sit, whose garment was white as snow, and the hair of his head like the pure wool: his throne was like the fiery flame, and his wheels as burning fire.
>
> 10 A fiery stream issued and came forth from before him: thousand thousands ministered unto him, and ten thousand times ten thousand stood before him: the judgment was set, and the books were opened.
>
> 11 I beheld then because of the voice of the great words which the horn spake: I beheld even till the beast was slain, and his body destroyed, and given to the burning flame.
>
> 12 As concerning the rest of the beasts, they had their dominion taken away: yet their lives were prolonged for a season and time.
>
> 13 I saw in the night visions, and, behold, one like the Son of man came with the clouds of heaven, and came to the Ancient of days, and they brought him near before him.
>
> 14 And there was given him dominion, and glory, and a kingdom, that all people, nations, and languages, should serve him: his dominion is an everlasting dominion, which shall not pass away, and his kingdom that which shall not be destroyed.

So according to this prophecy of Daniel, after the thrones and kingdoms of the Earth are destroyed, Adam (the Ancient of Days) will revisit the Earth at and his righteous posterity will be gathered before him. Christ will come down and the keys of the kingdom of the Earth will be returned to Him whose right it is to rule during the Millennium. This will take place at Adam-ondi-Ahman. Also among the sacred business of the day will be the partaking of the sacrament. Doctrine and Covenants 27:4-14 refers. (Smith, Doctrine and Covenants, 1844)

2 For, behold, I say unto you, that it mattereth not what ye shall eat or what ye shall drink when ye partake of the sacrament, if it so be that ye do it with an eye single to my glory—remembering unto the Father my body which was laid down for you, and my blood which was shed for the remission of your sins.

3 Wherefore, a commandment I give unto you, that you shall not purchase wine neither strong drink of your enemies;

4 Wherefore, you shall partake of none except it is made anew among you; yea, in this my Father's kingdom which shall be built up on the earth.

5 Behold, this is wisdom in me; wherefore, marvel not, for the hour cometh that I will drink of the fruit of the vine with you on the earth, and with Moroni, whom I have sent unto you to reveal the Book of Mormon, containing the fulness of my everlasting gospel, to whom I have committed the keys of the record of the stick of Ephraim;

6 And also with Elias, to whom I have committed the keys of bringing to pass the restoration of all things spoken by the mouth of all the holy prophets since the world began, concerning the last days;

7 And also John the son of Zacharias, which Zacharias he (Elias) visited and gave promise that he should have a son, and his name should be John, and he should be filled with the spirit of Elias;

8 Which John I have sent unto you, my servants, Joseph Smith, Jun., and Oliver Cowdery, to ordain you unto the first priesthood which you have received, that you might be called and ordained even as Aaron;

9 And also Elijah, unto whom I have committed the keys of the power of turning the hearts of the fathers to the children, and the hearts of the children to the fathers, that the whole earth may not be smitten with a curse;

10 And also with Joseph and Jacob, and Isaac, and Abraham, your fathers, by whom the promises remain;

11 And also with Michael, or Adam, the father of all, the prince of all, the ancient of days;

12 And also with Peter, and James, and John, whom I have sent unto you, by whom I have ordained you and confirmed you to be apostles, and especial witnesses of my name, and bear the keys of your ministry and of the same things which I revealed unto them;

13 Unto whom I have committed the keys of my kingdom, and a dispensation of the gospel for the last times; and for the fulness of times, in the which I will gather together in one all things, both which are in heaven, and which are on earth;

14 And also with all those whom my Father hath given me out of the world.

So all the righteous gathered there will partake of the sacrament with Christ the Lord.

There is a hymn written by William W Phelps about Adam-ondi-Ahman:

'This earth was once a garden place, With all her glories common, And men did live a holy race, And worship Jesus face to face, In Adam-ondi-Ahman.

We read that Enoch walk'd with God, Above the power of mammon, While Zion spread herself abroad, And Saints and angels sung aloud, In Adam-ondi-Ahman.

Her land was good and greatly blest, Beyond old Israel's Canaan; Her fame was known from east to west, Her peace was great, and pure the rest Of Adam-ondi-Ahman.

Hosannah to such days to come—The Saviour's second coming, When all the earth in glorious bloom, Affords the Saints a holy home, Like Adam-ondi-Ahman.'

Adam-ondi-Ahman was referred to during the prophet Joseph Smith Jr.'s time as Spring Hill and is located in Davies County, Missouri. Spring Hill is north of the valley of Adam-ondi-Ahman, through which runs the Grand River, described by the Prophet Joseph as a 'large, beautiful, deep and rapid stream, during the high waters of spring.' In the spring and summer the surrounding valley is most beautiful, with its scattered farms discernible as far as the eye can reach.

The most detailed description is found in a footnote in the History of the Church: (Roberts, 1902)

'Adam-ondi-Ahman, or "Diahman," as it is familiarly known to the Saints, is located on the north bank of Grand River. It is situated, in fact, in a sharp bend of that stream. The river comes sweeping down from the northwest and here makes a sudden turn and runs in a meandering course to the northeast for some two or three miles, when it as suddenly makes another bend and flows again to the southeast. Grand River is a stream that has worn a deep channel for itself, and left its banks precipitous; but at "Diahman" that is only true of the south bank. The stream as it rushes from the northwest, strikes the high prairie land which at this point contains beds of limestone, and not being able to cut its way through, it veered off to the northeast, and left that height of land standing like palisades which rise very abruptly from the stream to a height of from fifty to seventy-five feet. The summit of these bluffs is the common level of the high rolling prairie, extending off in the direction of Far West. The bluffs on the north bank recede some distance from the stream, so that the river bottom at this point widens out to a small valley. The bluffs on the north bank of the river are by no means as steep as those on the south, and are covered with a light growth of timber. A ridge runs out from the main line of the bluffs into the river bottom some two or three hundred yards, approaching the stream at the point where the bend of the river is made. The termination of the bluff is quite abrupt, and overlooks a considerable portion of the river bottom. . . . North of the ridge on which the ruins of the altar were found, and running parallel with it, is another ridge, separated from the first by a depression varying in width from fifty to a hundred yards. This small valley with the larger one through which flows the Grand River, is the valley of Adam-ondi-Ahman'.

Spring Hill is about fifty or sixty miles north and somewhat to the east of Independence, Missouri.

Elder Heber C. Kimball recalled being with the prophet in Davies County, Missouri, and described the experience as follows (Caldwell, 1982):

'The Prophet Joseph called upon Brother Brigham, myself and others, saying, "Brethren, come, go along with me, and I will show you something," He led us a short distance to a place where were the ruins of three altars built of stone, one above the other, and one standing a little back of the other, like unto the pulpits in the Kirtland Temple, representing the order of three grades of Priesthood; "There," said Joseph, "is the place where Adam offered up sacrifice after he was cast out of the garden." The altar stood at the highest point of the bluff. I went and examined the place several times while I remained there.'

Figure 23—The LDS Plaque at Adam-Ondi-Ahman

Figure 24—The Valley of Adam-ondi-Ahman

On a recent visit to Adam-ondi-Ahman, we came across the Galatin Ward building of the Church of Jesus Christ of LDS. Galatin is the nearest town to Adam-ondi-Ahman. The Ward building is very large and impressive when compared with the average ward building (see pictures):

Figure 25—The LDS Galatin Ward Building—Rear View

Figure 26—The LDS Galatin Ward Building—Front View

The current sacrament attendance at Galatin is around 250 and member families are moving into the area at around one family a week! Only a few years ago, there was only a branch in the area meeting in rented accommodation. So it seems that the area is being prepared for the events preceding the second coming by the strengthening of the Church presence in that area. In addition, the Church of Jesus Christ of Latter Day Saints has already purchased much of the farmland around Adam-ondi-Ahman. So the scene is set!

CH 16

THE NEW JERUSALEM

Joseph Smith taught that the City of Zion in the latter days will be at Independence in Jackson County, Missouri. The city will be called the New Jerusalem.

Moses 7:62 (Smith, The Pearl of Great Price, 1851)

> 62 And righteousness will I send down out of heaven; and truth will I send forth out of the earth, to bear testimony of mine Only Begotten; his resurrection from the dead; yea, and also the resurrection of all men; and righteousness and truth will I cause to sweep the earth as with a flood, to gather out mine elect from the four quarters of the earth, unto a place which I shall prepare, an Holy City, that my people may gird up their loins, and be looking forth for the time of my coming; for there shall be my tabernacle, and it shall be called Zion, a New Jerusalem.

This is also referred to in Doctrine and Covenants 57:1-4 (Smith, Doctrine and Covenants, 1844)

> 1 Hearken, O ye elders of my church, saith the Lord your God, who have assembled yourselves together, according to my commandments, in this land, which is the land of Missouri,

which is the land which I have appointed and consecrated for the gathering of the saints.

2 Wherefore, this is the land of promise, and the place for the city of Zion.

3 And thus saith the Lord your God, if you will receive wisdom here is wisdom. Behold, the place which is now called Independence is the centre place; and a spot for the temple is lying westward, upon a lot which is not far from the courthouse.

4 Wherefore, it is wisdom that the land should be purchased by the saints, and also every tract lying westward, even unto the line running directly between Jew and Gentile;

The early saints did indeed buy land in Independence and marked out a Temple lot. Joseph Smith directed the dedication of the Temple site by Sidney Rigdon on the 3rd August 1831 and Joseph laid a corner-marking stone. Bishop Edward Partridge purchased a 63-acre parcel of land, including the site for the Temple, on the 19th December 1831. However, the expulsion of Saints from Jackson County in November 1833 prevented the construction of the Temple. Eventually, the property including the Temple lot was sold with the approval of Brigham Young and other apostles on the 5th May 1848.

However, the Church of Jesus Christ of Latter Day Saints has subsequently purchased land covering part of the original Temple lot, as can be seen in Figure 27. The original Temple lot was the rough triangle marked out by Pacific St, Union St and Lexington St. The area containing 1 to 5 is now owned by the Church of Jesus Christ of Latter Day Saints, the area containing 6 to 8 by the Community of Christ (was Re-organised Church of Jesus Christ of LDS) and the number 9 part is owned by the Church of Christ (Temple Lot) who were called Hedrikites.

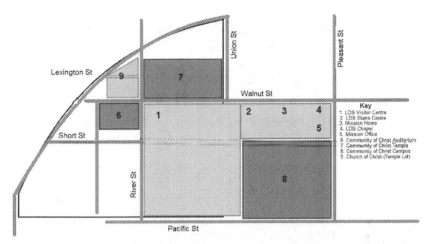

Figure 27—The Temple Lot in Independence, Missouri

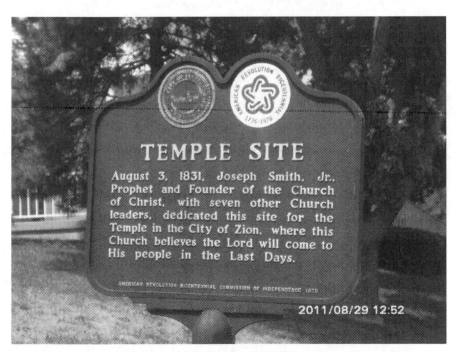

Figure 28—A Plaque which Marks the Independence Temple Site

The above plaque which marks the Independence Temple Site is on the vacant lot owned by the Church of Christ (Temple Lot).

The New Jerusalem will become a place of refuge for the righteous from the wars and strife that are present everywhere else in the world in the latter days. This will be after the governments of the world have been destroyed in the violent upheavals of nature that precede the second coming. Righteous saints from all the world will be gathered to this city (although it is not clear whether this means all righteous saints). Doctrine and Covenants 45:66-69 refers. (Smith, Doctrine and Covenants, 1844)

> 66 And it shall be called the New Jerusalem, a land of peace, a city of refuge, a place of safety for the saints of the Most High God;
>
> 67 And the glory of the Lord shall be there, and the terror of the Lord also shall be there, insomuch that the wicked will not come unto it, and it shall be called Zion.
>
> 68 And it shall come to pass among the wicked, that every man that will not take his sword against his neighbour must needs flee unto Zion for safety.
>
> 69 And there shall be gathered unto it out of every nation under heaven; and it shall be the only people that shall not be at war one with another.

Figure 29—The Community of Christ Temple in Independence

How will the saints be able to take possession of the lands in Missouri including the Temple lot? The scriptures speak of the violent upheavals that will precede the second coming and in particular they mention that the seas will heave beyond their bounds. Missouri is a low lying area and it could be that tidal waves will wipe the area clean of all inhabitants or some other destruction will do the same. Brigham Young as quoted by Heber C

Kimball said that when the saints returned to this area there would be no inhabitants to plague them. (Kimball, 1931)

"The Western boundary of the state of Missouri will be swept so clean of its inhabitants that as President Young tells us, when you return to that place, there will not be left so much as a yellow dog to wag its tail."

In addition, Orson Pratt made the following statement in 1875 on this subject. (Pratt O., 1875)

"when the time shall come that the Lord shall waste away this nation, he will give commandment to this people to return and possess their own inheritance which they purchased some forty-four years ago in the state of Missouri."

Those who gather to the New Jerusalem will have to be prepared to live as a 'Zion people', that is, they will have to live the law of consecration. When we read about the ancient City of Enoch which was taken up from this Earth because its people were so righteous, we learn the following. Moses 7:18-21 (Smith, The Pearl of Great Price, 1851)

> 18 And the Lord called his people ZION, because they were of one heart and one mind, and dwelt in righteousness; and there was no poor among them.
>
> 19 And Enoch continued his preaching in righteousness unto the people of God. And it came to pass in his days, that he built a city that was called the City of Holiness, even ZION.
>
> 20 And it came to pass that Enoch talked with the Lord; and he said unto the Lord: Surely Zion shall dwell in safety forever. But the Lord said unto Enoch: Zion have I blessed, but the residue of the people have I cursed.
>
> 21 And it came to pass that the Lord showed unto Enoch all the inhabitants of the earth; and he beheld, and lo, Zion, in process of time, was taken up into heaven. And the Lord said unto Enoch: Behold mine abode forever.

So the City of Enoch had no poor. Now the City of Enoch will descend to join the saints in the New Jerusalem, as confirmed in Moses 7:62-63. (Smith, The Pearl of Great Price, 1851)

> 62 And righteousness will I send down out of heaven; and truth will I send forth out of the earth, to bear testimony of

mine Only Begotten; his resurrection from the dead; yea, and also the resurrection of all men; and righteousness and truth will I cause to sweep the earth as with a flood, to gather out mine elect from the four quarters of the earth, unto a place which I shall prepare, an Holy City, that my people may gird up their loins, and be looking forth for the time of my coming; for there shall be my tabernacle, and it shall be called Zion, a New Jerusalem.

63 And the Lord said unto Enoch: Then shalt thou and all thy city meet them there, and we will receive them into our bosom, and they shall see us; and we will fall upon their necks, and they shall fall upon our necks, and we will kiss each other;

Thus the people of the City of Enoch will join with the people of the New Jerusalem and they will all live the same law of consecration and be a 'Zion' people. Many of the brethren have spoken on this subject, but two quotations will be sufficient. Lorenzo Snow said in Conference in 1898. (Snow, 1898)

"These are things for the Latter-day Saint and for every man and woman to think about, and we should commence to prepare and fit ourselves for the United Order. As far as spiritual things are concerned we are pretty well united, but when it comes to temporalities we often differ. But you will see the day, if you live properly, observe the Word of Wisdom and do that which is required, you will go back to Jackson county, many of you whom I am addressing this afternoon. I am sure of this."

Orson Pratt said. (Various, Journal of Discourses Vol 21, 1879, p. 149)

"You may ask, in what respect we shall differ in settling up those countries when we go there to fulfil the commandments of Lord? I will tell you. No man in those localities will be permitted to receive a stewardship on those lands, unless he is willing to consecrate all his properties to the Lord."

It is clear from these quotes that living the law of consecration will be a requirement of those who gather to the New Jerusalem. This will be necessary in order for them to become a 'Zion people' who are of one heart and one mind. As a result of the inhabitants of the city living this higher law and being righteous in all things, the City of Zion or New Jerusalem will enjoy the benefits of a terrestrial state rather than those of the telestial state which we now endure. This can be understood from the following statements by Orson Pratt. (Various, Journal of Discourses Vol 21, 1879)

"The cities and temples which we are now engaged in building, we expect to decay; we expect the rock and the various building materials will in time waste away, according to natural laws. But when we build that great eternal city, the New Jerusalem, there will be no such thing as the word decay associated with it; it will not decay any more than the pot of manna which was gathered by the children of Israel and put into a sacred place in the Ark of the Covenant. It was preserved from year to year by the power of God; so will he preserve the city of the New Jerusalem, the dwelling houses, the tabernacles, the Temples, etc., from the effects of storms and time."

And on another occasion, he said:

> "Therefore, Latter-day Saints, when you return to build up the waste places of Zion, and when you build up the New Jerusalem upon the place that he has appointed, whatever materials shall be used, by the blessing of the Priesthood, which God has ordained, these materials will endure forever: they will continue during the thousand years, without waste, and when they shall be caught up to heaven, when the earth flees away, they will still endure in all their perfection and beauty. When these cities shall descend again upon the new earth, in its immortal and eternal state, they will still be as endurable as the earth itself, no more to be subject to the curse, and therefore, will no more waste; death is gone—everything that is corruptible in its nature has ceased, so far as this habitable globe is concerned, and all sorrow and mourning are done away".

In the Millennium the Earth will be in a Terrestrial state and it would seem that the New Jerusalem will have an early preview of this state of existence.

CH 17

Silence for the Space of Half an Hour

When reading in the scriptures about the troubled times which will precede the second coming, there are two scriptures which are very thought provoking:

Revelation 8:1

And when he had opened the seventh seal, there was silence in heaven about the space of half an hour.

Doctrine and Covenants 88:95 (Smith, Doctrine and Covenants, 1844)

And there shall be silence in heaven for the space of half an hour; and immediately after shall the curtain of heaven be unfolded, as a scroll is unfolded after it is rolled up, and the face of the Lord shall be unveiled;

Both of these scriptures come after verses which describe the terrible calamities which will befall the Earth when its motion is disturbed prior to the second coming of Jesus Christ. What do they mean?

In the Lord's time, one day equals a thousand of our years. Half an hour, therefore, in the Lord's time will be about 20 years of our time. The implication is that, after a period of planetary upheavals, there will be a short period of time during which the heavens will be silent and no further calamities will occur. After that, there will be further calamities and then the Lord will appear in glory out of the East.

What is the purpose of this 'half an hour'? If it equates to about twenty of our years, one can reason that the initial calamities prior to this period will overthrow the kingdoms of the Earth and decimate the population of the Earth. Indeed this is not reasoning without evidence as a reference to modern scripture will show.

Doctrine and Covenants 87:6 (Smith, Doctrine and Covenants, 1844)

And thus, with the sword and by bloodshed the inhabitants of the earth shall mourn; and with famine, and plague, and earthquake, and the thunder of heaven, and the fierce and vivid lightning also, shall the inhabitants of the earth be made to feel the wrath, and indignation, and chastening hand of an Almighty God, until the consumption decreed hath made a full end of all nations;

Thus we see that calamities which mankind shall suffer at this time will be such as to 'make a full end of all nations' leaving the way clear for the Saviour to come down to Earth in glory and take His rightful place as King and ruler of all. However, prior to that glorious event, there will exist an environment in which the Lord's faithful saints can migrate to the New Jerusalem in Missouri and build the holy city and Temple there ready for the advent of the Saviour. Also, the Jews in Jerusalem will be able to take possession of the Temple Mount and rebuild the Temple there also in preparation for the Saviour's coming. Outside of these areas, the world will become a wild and desperate place with little law and order and even less food or permanent shelter. Neighbour will raise the sword against neighbour and bands of desperadoes will roam the Earth. There will be no peace outside Zion. The great cities of the Earth will have been destroyed by the convulsions of nature and conditions will be such that some will wonder whether any of mankind will survive the cataclysms of nature. Even some of the faithful will wonder whether Christ is delaying his coming too long.

Doctrine and Covenants 45:26 (Smith, Doctrine and Covenants, 1844)

And in that day shall be heard of wars and rumours of wars, and the whole earth shall be in commotion, and men's hearts shall fail them, and they shall say that Christ delayeth his coming until the end of the earth.

One interpretation of this scripture is that some will fear that the Earth and its inhabitants will be totally destroyed before Christ returns the second time. Their concerns will not be without cause for the Lord himself stated that these times have had to be shortened for the sake of the elect. In the Bible we can read:

Mark 13:20

And except that the Lord had shortened those days, no flesh should be saved: but for the elect's sake, whom he hath chosen, he hath shortened the days.

So the chosen of the Lord need not worry, for their sake the Lord will shorten the days of calamity such that they can and will survive as a people to witness the Saviour's second advent.

After the Saints and the Jews complete their preparations, there will probably be some further upheavals and then the Saviour will appear on the Mount of Olives in Jerusalem. (He will of course have already appeared by then to the faithful in Adam-Ondi-Ahman).

Marc Udall in his book about the revelations of St John (Udall, 1996), suggested that Christ's ministry took place in the fourth seal, that being the meridian of time. Thus three seals would be opened on each side of the ministry and the fifth seal would be opened after his death in around AD34. This in turn suggests that the opening of the seventh seal (i.e. the time of Christ's second coming) will be around AD2034 or so. It is worthwhile noting that a period of calm of around fifteen or twenty years after the upheavals which will destroy the kingdoms of the world will, if those upheavals are imminent as this book suggests, take us to around AD 2035 for the second coming. These dates should be understood to be an approximate scheme of events and not to be interpreted as exact dates for the events. (No man knoweth the hour!).

CH 18

The Millennium

In the Millennium the Earth will be in a Terrestrial state with all the benefits that will bring. There will be no sickness, crime or decay. Food will be plentiful and free from pests and disease. The lion will lie down with the lamb and wars will cease. The Earth will be restored to its paradisiacal glory and Christ the Lord will rule over the Earth through his servants.

Two Jerusalems are referred to in the Millennium, the Old and the New. Ether refers to this in the Book of Mormon. Ether 13:4-6. (Smith, The Book of Mormon, 1830)

> 4 Behold, Ether saw the days of Christ, and he spake concerning a New Jerusalem upon this land.
>
> 5 And he spake also concerning the house of Israel, and the Jerusalem from whence Lehi should come—after it should be destroyed it should be built up again, a holy city unto the Lord; wherefore, it could not be a new Jerusalem for it had been in a time of old; but it should be built up again, and become a holy city of the Lord; and it should be built unto the house of Israel—
>
> 6 And that a New Jerusalem should be built up upon this land, unto the remnant of the seed of Joseph, for which things there has been a type.

Ether, of course, was on the American continent at the time of his prophesy so when he says 'this land' he means the American continent. In Isaiah 2:3 we read.

> 3 And many people shall go and say, Come ye, and let us go up to the mountain of the LORD, to the house of the God of Jacob; and he will teach us of his ways, and we will walk in his paths: for out of Zion shall go forth the law, and the word of the LORD from Jerusalem.

So it would appear that the law and administration will be done from the New Jerusalem and spiritual direction will be done from the Old Jerusalem.

The great work of the Millennial period will be genealogy. All the records that the members of the Church of Jesus Christ of Latter Day Saints are currently collecting and collating will be joined with the records kept in the spirit world and a complete record for all people back to Adam will be compiled. This will be a great work which will involve many people for many years. In addition all the outstanding Temple work for the individuals in the record so compiled will need to be done. Again this will need substantial effort on the part of those living in the Millennium. Brigham Young said: (Various, Journal of Discourses Vol 6, 1859)

"When his kingdom is established upon the earth, and Zion built up, the Lord will send his servants as saviours upon Mount Zion. The servants of God who have lived on the earth in ages past will reveal where different persons have lived who have died without the Gospel, give their names, and say, 'Now go forth, ye servants of God, and exercise your rights and privileges;· go and perform the ordinances of the house of God for those who have passed their probation without the law, and for all who will receive any kind of salvation: bring them up to inherit, the celestial, terrestrial, and telestial kingdoms'".

How wonderful it will be for those living on the Earth in the Millennium to interact with resurrected beings! All this emphasis on work for the dead will require that many Temples are built in order to accommodate all the work that will be required. John Taylor said: (Various, Journal of Discourses Vol 25, 1884)

"This is at great work. Well might it be said to Joseph Smith, 'You are laying the foundation of a great work'—so vast that very few can begin to comprehend it. We read sometimes about the millennium, but what do we know about it? It is a time when this work will be going on, and Temples, thousands of them, will be reared for the accomplishment of the objects designed, in which communications from the heavens will be received in regard to our labours, how we may perform them, and for whom."

Wilford Woodruff further said: (Various, Journal of Discourses Vol 19, 1877)

When the Saviour comes, a thousand years will be devoted to this work of redemption; and Temples will appear all over this land of Joseph,—North: and South America—and also in Europe and elsewhere; and all the descendants of Shem, Ham, and Japheth who received not the Gospel in the flesh, must be officiated for in the Temples of God, before the Saviour can present the kingdom to the Father, saying, "It is finished."

Thus many of those on the Earth at that time will be fully involved in this work.

Joseph Smith laid out a plan for the city of New Jerusalem. It is likely that the building of the city will follow that plan which consisted of blocks as do most US cities. The great Temple complex which will be in the centre of the New Jerusalem was also described. Orson Pratt recorded the details as follows (pp24-25). (Various, Journal of Discourses Vol 24, 1879(2))

"There will be 24—different compartments in the Temple that will be built in Jackson County. The names of these compartments were given to us some 45 or 46 years ago; the names we still have and when we build these 24 rooms, in a circular form and arched over the centre, we shall give the names to all these different compartments just as the Lord specified through Joseph Smith . . . Perhaps you may ask for what purposes these 24 compartments are to be built. I answer not to assemble the outside world in, nor to assemble the Saints all in one place, but these buildings will be built with a special view to the different orders, or in other words the different quorums or councils of the two Priesthoods that God has ordained on the earth. That is the object of having 24 rooms so that each of these different quorums, whether they be High Priests, or Seventies, or Elders, or Bishops, or lesser Priesthood, or Teachers, or Deacons, or Patriarchs, or Apostles, or High Councils, or whatever may be the duties that are assigned to them, they will have rooms in the Temple of the Most High God, adapted, set apart, constructed, and dedicated for this special purpose. Now, I have not only told you that we shall have these rooms, but I have told you the object of these rooms in short, not in full. But will there be any other buildings excepting those 24 rooms that are all joined together in a circular form and arched over the centre—are there any other rooms that will be built—detached from the Temple? Yes. There will be tabernacles, there will be meeting houses for the assembling of the people on the Sabbath day. There will be various places of meeting so that the people may gather together; but the Temple will be dedicated to the Priesthood of the Most High God, and for most sacred and holy purposes."

It seems that the Temple complex will not only provide accommodation for Temple ordinances but also for the administration of Priesthood quorums. It will probably house rooms to accommodate family history administration also.

CH 19

Conclusion

So the principal directions of the Great Pyramid are synchronising with significant stars at this time for the first time since 2450 BC. In addition, the constellation of Orion rises to its zenith and points to the junction of the ecliptic and the galactic equator just as the solstice sun rises at that point. It has not done so for at least 25,830 years (if ever!). Orion, we learn, symbolises Jesus Christ and is probably a sign of the Son of Man rising. This happens just as the constellation of Draco the dragon, which symbolises the devil, arrives at its lowest point in the sky and stays there for around 1000 years. The painted ceiling in the tomb of Seti I suggests that this position of Orion is a harbinger of a change in the Earth's orbit, with all the devastation that such an occurrence would cause.

Meanwhile, the Shepherd Stone of Israel (or the Stone of Destiny) has been moved from its position in Westminster Abbey. This is subsequent to its third overthrow as prophesied in the Bible. The Jews at Jerusalem have prepared vessels and priests for a third Temple. A kosher tenth red heifer has been bred and the Jews are thus ready to build a new Temple at Jerusalem and perform ordinances and offer offerings in it. Israel continues to overstep the mark in its own defence in the view of the United Nations. Will the situation with Iran prove to be its undoing?

Finally, the Church of Jesus Christ of Latter Day Saints owns much land at Adam-ondi-Ahman and the local Ward of Galatin is strengthening rapidly.

These signs above are in addition to the more usual signs of the second coming which many others have spoken about (e.g. wars and rumours of wars, famine and pestilence, false Christs, great wickedness, the Church of Jesus Christ going into all the world, etc).

What do we conclude from all this? Whilst no one knoweth the hour of the second coming, the indications are that the tribulations which will precede the second coming are imminent and will probably commence within the next decade or so. We should all follow the counsel of the Lord's prophets and prepare ourselves well, both spiritually and temporally.

Finally, I can do no better than quote Wilford Woodruff (Woodruff, 1840):

> 'I now take the liberty, through the channel of the press, to invite all . . . into whose hands these lines may fall, that have not already obeyed the fullness of the gospel of Jesus Christ, to repent of all their sins, and be baptized in water for the remission of their sins, that they may receive the gift of the Holy Ghost by the laying on of hands,—that they may have upon them the wedding garment, that their lamps may be trimmed and burning, and be prepared to go forth and meet the Bridegroom, who is at the door—for the day when the Lord Jesus shall cleanse the Earth, by the spirit of judgement and the spirit of burning, from sin, wickedness, and pollution, until it becomes a fit abode for the Saviour to dwell upon, and reign one thousand years with his Saints.'

BIBLIOGRAPHY

Bauval, G. a. (1994). The Orion Mystery. W Heinemann Ltd.

Benson, E. T. (1987, November). Ensign, p. 4.

Brough, R. C. (1979). The Lost Tribes. Horizon.

Caldwell, O. a. (1982). Sacred Truths of The Doctrine and Covenants.

Cowley, M. F. (1964). Wilford Woodruff. Bookcraft.

Dechend, d. S. (1969). Hamlet's Mill. Gambit.

Hilton, L. M. (2006). The Kolob Theorem. Granite Publishing and Distribution.

Ivins, A. W. (n.d.). The Lost Tribes.

Jueneman, F. (1975). Limits of Uncertainty. Done-Donnelly.

Kimball, H. C. (1931, May 23rd). Deseret News, p. 3.

Larson, A. E. (1985). And There Shall be a New Heaven and a New Earth. Zedek.

Lockyer, N. (1894). The Dawn of Astronomy. Macmillan.

Ludlow, D. H. (1991). The Encyclopedia of Mormonism Vol 1. McMillan.

Lundy, J. P. (1876). Monumental Christianity: Or, The Art and Symbolism of the Primitive Church. J W Bouton, NY.

Massey, G. (1907). Ancient Egypt, The Light of the World. TF Unwin.

McConkie, B. R. (1982). The Millenial Messiah. Deseret Book Co.

Mendelssohn, K. (1974). The Riddle of The Pyramids. Thames and Hudson.

Milner W.M.H. (1991) The Royal House of Britain. Covenant Publishing

Murdock, D. M. (2009). Christ in Egypt. Stellar House.

Nibley, H. (1975). The Message of the Joseph Smith Papyri. Deseret Book Co.

O'Connor, R. (1822). the Chronicles of Eri. London: Phillips.

Penrose, C. W. (1859, Sept). The Second Advent. Millenial Star, pp. Vol 21 pp 582-3.

Pratt, O. (1875, October 2nd). Deseret Evening News, p. 1.

Pratt, P. P. (1837). A Voice of Warning. Kirtland: The Church of Jesus Christ of Latter Day Saints.

Roberts, B. H. (1902). History of The Church of Jesus Christ Of Latter Day Saints. Deseret Book Co.

Smith, J. (1830). The Book of Mormon. Salt Lake City: Church of Jesus Christ of Latter Day Saints.

Smith, J. (1844). Doctrine and Covenants. Church of Jesus Christ of Latter Day Saints.

Smith, J. (1844). Joseph Smith Papers. (p. July 19th 1840). Salt Lake City: Church of Jesus Christ of Latter Day Saints.

Smith, J. (1851). The Pearl of Great Price. Church of Jesus Christ of Latter Day Saints.

Smith, J. (1976). Teachings of the Prophet Joseph Smith. Deseret Book Co.

Smythe, C. P. (1877). Our Inheritance in the Great Pyramid. London.

Snow, L. (1898). April Conference Church of Jesus Christ of Latter Day Saints (p. 14). Salt Lake City: Church of Jesus Christ of Latter Day Saints.

Talbot, D. N. (1980). The Saturn Myth. Doubleday and Co.

Udall, M. R. (1996). The Patience of The Saints:A Hypothesis Based on The Revelations of John The Beloved. Lindon, Utah: BYU.

Various. (1855). Journal of Discourses Vol 2. Salt Lake City: Church of Jesus Christ of Latter Day Saints.

Various. (1859). Journal of Discourses Vol 6. Salt Lake City: Church of Jesus Christ of Latter Day Saints.

Various. (1877). Journal of Discourses Vol 19. Salt Lake City: Church of Jesus Christ of Latter Day Saints.

Various. (1879). Journal of Discourses Vol 21. Salt Lake City: Church of Jesus Christ of Latter Day Saints.

Various. (1879). Journal of Discourses Vol 21.

Various. (1879(2)). Journal of Discourses Vol 24. Salt Lake City: The Church of Jesus Christ of Latter Day Saints.

Various. (1881). Journal of Discourses Vol 23. Salt Lake City: Church of Jesus Christ of Latter Day Saints.

Various. (1884). Journal of Discourses Vol 25. Salt Lake City: Church of Jesus Christ of Latter Day Saints.

Verner, M. (2001). The Pyramids. Grove/Atlantic.

Vidler, M. (1998). The Star Mirror. Thorsons.

Walker, W. (1999). In The Isles of The Sea. Trafford Publishing.

Witt, R. E. (1997). Isis in the Ancient World. J Hopkins University Press.

Woodruff, W. (1840, August). Millennial Star.

Myers P.V.N. (1916) Ancient History, Ginn and Co

INDEX